A Comeback Begins in Earnest

It was old-fashioned training, the way it used to be—no crowds, no frills, just riding and more riding. Lance went out every day and rode in all kinds of weather. The experience brought Lance back to earlier days and he began to just enjoy the act of riding hard, of feeling his body tire, of working against the elements and pressing on. In the evenings the men ate and talked and laughed about old times, all the things that had brought Lance so close to the pinnacle of his sport before his illness had struck. Going to North Carolina was almost like going back in time, when things were much simpler, when Lance would get on his bike and attack, just one man against everyone else. . . .

Also by BILL GUTMAN

Tiger Woods: A Biography

LANCE ARMSTRONG

ARMSTRONG

A BIOGRAPHY

BILL GUTMAN

Simon Pulse
New York   London   Toronto   Sydney

SIMON PULSE

An imprint of Simon & Schuster Children's Publishing Division
1230 Avenue of the Americas, New York, NY 10020
Copyright © 2003, 2005 by Bill Gutman
All rights reserved, including the right of reproduction in whole or in part in any form.
SIMON PULSE and colophon are registered trademarks of Simon & Schuster, Inc.
Designed by Ann Zeak
The text of this book was set in AGaramond.
Manufactured in the United States of America
This Simon Pulse edition October 2005
10 9 8 7 6 5 4 3 2
Library of Congress Control Number 2005932086
ISBN-13: 978-1-4169-1797-7
ISBN-10: 1-4169-1797-7

To all those people battling a serious illness or
other seemingly insurmountable adversity:
There is always hope.

Table of Contents

Introduction

At first it was the proverbial feel-good story. An athlete comes back from a near-fatal illness to return to his sport. Then he becomes a champion, winning the sport's biggest event, something he couldn't do before becoming ill. And when he triumphs again and again and again— seven times in all—he writes one of the greatest sports stories of all time.

The athlete is Lance Armstrong and the event the Tour de France, a three-week-long cycling race that covers more than two thousand miles. Its various stages take riders through the Alps and Pyrenees mountains. The Tour is widely considered the most demanding, debilitating, and grueling sports event in the world, and is the crown jewel of cycling, a race that Europeans have traditionally dominated throughout the years. Then along came Armstrong, who began forging a reputation in the cycling world but was never a real threat to win the Tour. That is, until cancer almost cost him his life.

Diagnosed with testicular cancer in 1996 at the age of twenty-five, Lance's life not only changed, it almost ended. Tests soon showed that the cancer had spread to his lungs and brain. His doctors, at the time, gave him a 40 percent chance of survival. Years later, those same doctors said they were being generous. Some felt Lance had no more than a 15 percent chance to live. But he fought back. He found doctors who would utilize a combination of chemotherapy drugs that would not damage his lungs, so he might ride again, and vowed to fight his illness to the end.

His ordeal was long and difficult, but eventually he began to recover. Miraculously, the combination of drugs worked and his body was declared cancer free. By then, Lance Armstrong was already back on his bike and thinking about a return to competition. He began focusing on the one race that gave him problems before his illness: the Tour de France.

Why is the Tour de France considered by so

many as the world's most grueling sports event? For argument's sake, let's compare the Tour with another event that takes tremendous conditioning and endurance: the Ironman triathlon. The Ironman is a one-day event in which competitors begin by swimming 2.4 miles. As soon as they come out of the water, they jump on bicycles and pedal for 112 miles. Once they complete that phase, they get off the bike, change their shoes, and begin running a 26.2-mile marathon—with no rest. Top competitors finish the three phases of the race in little more than eight hours. The Ironman is a test of conditioning, endurance, and will. But how does it measure up against the Tour de France?

With the Tour, not only do riders cover more than two thousand miles and ride up tortuously steep mountains, but they do it day after day. One stage ends, and after a few hours rest the next begins. For three weeks these elite cyclists must ride every day, often in scorching heat, in wind and rain, at high speeds, and always facing the possibility of a dangerous crash. Many riders have failed to finish the Tour, dropping out at various stages.

This happened to Lance Armstrong early in his career. In fact, he was told by his own advisors that he didn't have the body type to win the Tour. He was too big, too muscular, and too heavy for those long, uphill mountain climbs. After recovering from cancer, however, Lance's body had changed. He was about twenty pounds lighter and mountain riding became his forte. Once he excelled at the hills, he was tailor-made for the Tour de France.

"When I came back [from cancer]," Lance explained, "I said, 'If I ever get a chance to do this, I'm going to give it everything. I'm going to train correctly, eat right, and not going to mess up.' That's why I say all the time that the illness is the best thing that ever happened to me. I would never have won one Tour de France if I hadn't had [cancer]. No doubt."

His first Tour victory in 1999 was miraculous enough, but from there he went on to dominate the event as no one had before. Only one rider, Miguel Indurain of Spain, had won as many as five consecutive Tours. Lance Armstrong would win seven straight Tours before his retirement after the 2005 race. He has not only been an incredible athlete, but an inspiration to cancer patients and survivors the world over. The creation of the Lance Armstrong Foundation and his trademark LIVESTRONG yellow bracelets are just two of the ways he helps inspire people and raise money for cancer research. With all his great athletic achievements, Lance Armstrong has always been about giving back.

Competing in a sport that is barely a dot on the map in the United States, Lance has become a full-fledged sports celebrity, a guy who had all eyes in American turning toward France each July for seven years. Both sports fans and nonfans alike wanted to know how Lance was doing on the Tour. The answer was always the same: *He's winning and he won!*

Even today Lance Armstrong considers himself first and foremost a cancer survivor. To that end, he continues to inspire countless others, both directly and indirectly, and in that respect has become not only a sports icon, but a true American hero. His story is widely known, his achievements almost legendary. The strange bedfellows associated with his name will always be *cancer* and the *Tour de France*. Ironically, had he been just a champion cyclist with maybe one or two Tour wins, America would hardly have noticed.

But they sure do now.

1

The Beginnings of an Athletic Life

There was very little about Lance Armstrong's beginnings that would suggest a future Tour de France champion. But then again, there is very little about any young American boy that would suggest that. Sure, nearly all kids ride bicycles, but more of them will gravitate toward riding BMX bikes and doing tricks than going out-of-bounds on mountain bikes. Racing generally isn't an option unless it's BMX racing over rough terrain, full of bumps and jumps. Add that to the very difficult circumstances Lance was born into, and there wouldn't have seemed to be any kind of blueprint for athletic success.

He was born on September 18, 1971, in

Oak Cliff, Texas, a suburb of Dallas, to a single mother. Her maiden name was Linda Mooneyham and she was just seventeen at the time Lance was born. His father had already left; Lance wouldn't even know who he was for many years. Even after he found out, he said he had no interest in meeting him because there had never been any kind of connection between them. Fortunately, Lance's mother was a very special kind of person who could overcome hardship and was determined to raise her son to the best of her ability. They forged a close bond early on, a bond which remains very strong to this day.

Linda Mooneyham and her son lived in a one-bedroom apartment in Oak Cliff while she worked several part-time jobs and also finished high school. When she finally got a secretarial job, she began making more money and moved with her young son to another suburb north of Dallas called Richardson. She continued to work hard trying to make a better life for herself and Lance, and would later get a job with a telecommunications company and eventually obtain a real-estate license on the side. She is living proof that, through hard work and perseverance, a single mother can make a good life for herself and her child.

When Lance was three, his life changed

again. His mother married a man named Terry Armstrong who would soon legally adopt his stepson, giving him his last name. But Lance wasn't always happy with his stepfather. Terry Armstrong was a tough disciplinarian who wasn't averse to punishing Lance, sometimes for little things. He also used a paddle on occasions, something Lance doesn't remember too fondly. Because of these things, he never forged any kind of close bond with his stepfather.

Then when he was seven, he got his first bike. The family was still living in Richardson then and there was a store across the street from their apartment called the Richardson Bike Mart. The owner was a man named Jim Hoyt who often sponsored bicycle races. Hoyt loved the sport and also took pleasure in introducing young riders to racing. He got to know Lance and his mother, liked them, and finally gave her a deal on what Lance would call his first serious bike, a Schwinn Mag Scrambler. Lance loved it from the first.

He said having the bike represented "independence . . . freedom to roam without rules and without adults." So, if things weren't so good at home with his stepfather, Lance had his bike and could ride. Around this time the family moved again. Doing well at her job, and with a second paycheck coming in from her husband, Linda Armstrong was able to buy a house in nearby Plano, Texas, which was considered an upscale suburb of Dallas.

Even then, Lance had the ability to see things as they were. At first glance, he said it appeared to be the perfect American suburb, but he felt the place had no tradition and that nothing was real. People were very conscious of their status and the poorer people were looked down upon. Like so many other places in Texas, when it came to sports in Plano, football was king. As Lance said, "If you didn't play football, you didn't exist."

Naturally, any kid trying to fit in would try to play football. Lance tried, but soon found he didn't have the proper coordination for the sport. He admitted that he simply wasn't good at any sport that involved a ball, hand-eye coordination, and moving from side to side. Yet he had an athletic mentality, the tenacity needed to compete, and he desperately wanted to find something at which he could be successful. His first taste of athletic success came in a sport where nothing was needed but his own ability to move his body—running.

It began when he was in the fifth grade. That's when his elementary school announced a distance-running race and he entered. Before it started, Lance told his mother he was going to win. Sure enough, he got out front and, with all the determination he could muster, held on and crossed the finish line first. Winning was a new kind of feeling for him, and he liked it. Soon after, he joined a local swim club. At first, he wasn't very good and had to practice with younger kids. It didn't come easily. He worked and worked, and by the time he was twelve, he was a member of the City of Plano Swim Club.

Suddenly, Lance was becoming a very good swimmer. He had a fine coach in Chris MacCurdy, who worked very hard with him, and within a year of joining, he finished fourth in the state in the 1500-meter freestyle in his age group. He seemed to take to sports that required endurance and tenacity. In fact, it was with the Plano Swim Club that he began to develop his tremendous work ethic. He would work out with the swim club from five-thirty to seven A.M. before going to school, and work out again in the afternoon. To add another kind of training, he always rode his bike to and from school, a distance of ten miles each way. So he was swimming some six miles a day and biking twenty. Not bad for a young kid trying to get into shape. And all the while, he was becoming more and more of a quality athlete.

Soon after that, he discovered a sport that seemed a natural for his talents. He was about thirteen when he spotted a flyer for a competition called IronKids. It was a junior triathlon, and combined swimming, bike riding, and running. Young Lance couldn't believe his eyes.

"I had never heard of a triathlon before," he said, "but it was all the things I was good at, so I signed up."

It seemed a natural for him, a combination of three sports, all requiring great endurance, and all sports at which he had practiced or simply taken to, and at which he had begun to excel. He got himself the proper clothing and his first racing bike—a Mercier—which he described as a slim, elegant road bike, and jumped into his first triathlon with no previous experience or specific training. He won the event easily. Soon after, he entered a second triathlon in Houston and won again. Suddenly, Lance felt very good about himself. He had some athletic success at swimming, but had never been the best at anything. Before long, he was the best junior triathlete in the entire state of Texas.

"I liked the feeling," he said, simply and definitively.

What he found out about himself during those first triathlons was that the sport was almost a battle of attrition. Several athletes might have the same skill level, but the one

6

with the will to win, the one willing to push himself with total disregard to how he felt and the strain he was putting on his body, would win. Lance Armstrong soon felt that in this type of event, one where he could grit his teeth and absorb the punishment, he could outlast anyone and win.

A short time after finding his first real sports success, Lance had to deal with another crisis. When he was fourteen, his mother told him she would be asking Terry Armstrong for a divorce. Lance had never really liked his stepfather and didn't hide the fact that he was very happy about it. He made it clear a short time later that he didn't want to continue any kind of relationship with the man who had given him his name. He and his mother now grew closer than ever. No matter what else had happened, they always had each other.

Soon Lance began to concentrate even more on his growing athletic prowess. When he was just fifteen, he entered the 1987 President's Triathlon in Lake Levon, California, where he would be competing against many older and more experienced athletes. There would be no Cinderella-story finish here; Lance didn't win. But he still got a great deal of publicity by finishing 32nd in an experienced field. He was a kid competing against men; he had held up well. In races against competitors his own age, he was already picking up significant prize money. He was really beginning to feel his oats and went so far as to tell a reporter: "I think in a few years I'll be right near the top, and within ten years I'll be the best."

For young Lance, triathlons were a way to achieve the kind of success he craved, as well as a way to make some money that would help his mother. He began entering both events for his own age group and events where he competed against men, even if it meant fudging his birthdate on the entry forms. Competitors in men's events had to be at least sixteen. He won many of the age-group races, and sometimes placed in the top five in the other events. Either way, he was earning money and a reputation as a young triathlete on the rise. It seemed, at this point, that Lance Armstrong had found his sport.

Because he was a youngster with boundless energy, Lance soon began competing in some local bicycle races as well. He rode for his old friend Jim Hoyt, the man from whom he had bought his first bike. Hoyt sponsored a club team that competed in multi-lap road races around the fields that encircled the Richardson Bike Mart. Before long, Lance was winning those races. As with triathlons, he always gave it everything he had, pedaling until he felt his lungs would burst and his legs would move no longer. If there was another competitor to pass or a finish line in sight, he simply wouldn't quit or slow down.

Lance was so good that he quickly advanced to the age groups above his. When he was sixteen he was already riding against cyclists in their mid to late twenties. At sixteen, he also became the National Rookie of the Year in sprint triathlons and was earning some twenty thousand dollars a year. Even his mother now felt he had a future as an athlete and helped him every way she could. Lance continued to train in earnest, sometimes entering ten-kilometer runs just to improve his overall conditioning and endurance. When school was in session, he would run six miles right after school and in the evening hop on his bike for a long ride. On Saturdays his long rides would sometimes take him nearly to the Oklahoma border, and his mother would have to get in the car and go get him.

Riding all over the area on his bike wasn't always the safest situation for Lance. One time, after being run off the road by a truck, Lance made an obscene gesture. The trucker came after him, forcing Lance off his bike. He took off by foot only to see the trucker trashing his bike. Because he got the license number, Lance and his mother were able to take the trucker to court and win the case. Meanwhile, he got himself a new bike. This one was a Raleigh with racing wheels. A short time after getting the Raleigh, however, Lance wrecked it and almost got killed in the process.

He recalls riding in town and doing the dangerous practice of running stoplights, going through them one after another in an attempt to beat the timers. He had gone through five without incident when he came to an intersection that had six lanes. The light turned yellow and Lance started through at full speed. He remembers getting across the first three lanes but as he raced across the fourth, he saw a Ford Bronco out of the corner of his eye. The driver didn't see him and accelerated. The Bronco slammed right into the bike, sending Lance flying out of the seat and flying headfirst across the intersection. He landed on his head in what had to be a very frightening sight for those who witnessed it.

As unbelievable as it sounds, Lance was not wearing a helmet. In addition, he didn't even have identification with him. These are two things bike riders should *never* be without. The ID is especially needed when a rider is alone. Lance was taken to a hospital where it was determined that he had a concussion, plus he needed stitches to close gashes in his head and foot. He also had a sprained knee and, of course, a trashed bike. Needless to say, once his mother found out what had happened, she was extremely upset.

Lance, however, was upset about something else. He had been training for a triathlon that was to be held in six days at Lake Dallas, in Lewisville. His heart sank when he heard the doctor say there was absolutely no way he could compete. "Don't do anything for three weeks," the doctor ordered. "Don't run. Don't even walk."

The next day Lance was out of the hospital. He was limping badly and his whole body was sore from the impact of the crash. Within a couple of days, however, he had cabin fever and had to get out of the house. He played some golf, took the brace off his knee and felt pretty good. Just four days after the accident, Lance signed up to compete in the triathlon. He arranged to borrow a bike from a friend, actually took the stitches out of his foot himself, cut holes in his shoes so they wouldn't rub on the cut, and went to work. He was leading the race in the water and still leading when he got off the bike. In the 10K finishing run, he faded a bit and was passed by two other competitors, eventually finishing third.

Yet he got plenty of publicity for his accomplishment. There was a big newspaper story about how he had competed successfully so soon after being seriously injured in an accident. His determination turned a lot of heads, including that of the doctor who had patched him up. A week after the race, Lance and his mother received a letter from the doctor, which said, in part, "I can't believe it."

It wouldn't be the last time that Lance Armstrong would amaze the sporting world and doctors alike.

2
A Champion in the Making

Lance was pretty much a wild guy during his high school years. Though he didn't play football, he was still popular and had plenty of friends. Just as he liked fast sports, he also liked fast, "muscle" cars, and often drag-raced with his buddies. Like any athlete who seems to revel in speed, there was an element of danger in much of what he did. The accident he had while running yellow lights proved that, but he enjoyed the risks and wasn't about to slow down. It was life in the fast lane, and Lance felt he was heading toward something special.

That feeling soon became the primary motivation in his life. He had reached a point where he wasn't about to skip training to attend a football rally or even to hang out with his friends. Training, competing, and improving in the sports he had chosen—sports still considered "weird" by many of his peers—had become more important than anything else. It wasn't long before Lance's dedication began to pay off. In the fall of 1988, his senior year in high school, Lance really began to give the cycling world a glimpse of things to come. He entered a time-trial race in Moriarty, New Mexico. It was considered a very big race for young riders.

The race was twelve miles over a very flat course along a highway, in an area with very little wind. It was tailor-made for speed. In other words, it was the kind of race where riders could record fast times and hope that potential sponsors and others within the cycling world would notice them. In that sense, it was a very important race, and Lance, like the other entrants, wanted to excel. The race was held in September. The weather was still hot in Texas, but when Lance and his mother arrived in New Mexico, the air was cold, almost frigid. Because he hadn't packed any cold-weather clothing, Lance wasn't sure he could ride.

He took a forty-five-minute warm-up ride wearing his mother's thin windbreaker, but when he reached the starting area to wait his turn, he was still cold. In a time trial, riders are staggered so that each has a chance to make the ride by himself. It's strictly a matter of the rider against the clock; no strategy, no chance of colliding with another rider—just an all-out sprint for twelve miles. So Lance began waiting for his turn. He knew that if his body was cold when he started, chances were it would cost him valuable time. Instead of waiting outside, he got in his mother's car and had her turn the heat up. He sat there until his name was called. Then he jumped right on his bike and went.

Lance rode with the single-mindedness that would always characterize his style in this type of race. He was focused on one thing, going as fast as he could for as long as he could. He worked as hard as he could, ignored the pain, gave away nothing. When he finally crossed the finish line, exhausted, he had not only won the race, he had also broken the course record by an amazing forty-five seconds!

The victory in the Moriarty time trial seemed to complete his metamorphosis. Lance was now fully focused on becoming a world-class athlete, and cycling was becoming the sport in which he felt he could really excel. He began training even harder. Most everything else had become secondary, which was quite unusual for a high-school-age athlete. High schoolers who feel they have a future in base-ball, basketball, football, or other sports may work hard, but they know they will get more experience at a higher level in college or in the minor leagues, so their lives in high school are often pretty normal. Cycling is different. It is up to the athlete to make it happen. There is no high school team, no college scholarship wait-ing, and no minor league. The athlete has to do it on his own. That was the way Lance saw it; in his mind, that was the only way it could be viewed.

Lance was now taking long, solitary bike rides. There wasn't a lot of time for fun and games with his friends. Then, after the first of the year in what would be his final semester in high school, another opportunity came along. Word of his growing talent had spread, and the United States Cycling Federation invited him to travel to Colorado Springs to train with the U.S. Junior National Team and then travel to Moscow in Russia for the 1989 Junior World Championships. It was an incredible opportu-nity, but it didn't take long for a problem to develop.

Plano East High School had a policy regard-ing long absences. Lance was told if he went to Moscow he might not qualify to graduate with his class. Though he was disappointed at the stance the school had taken, Lance knew he couldn't pass up the opportunity. He had to go. The trip turned out to be a learning experience in more ways than one.

Up to this point, Lance knew only one way to ride. Attack! That was his credo. Go as hard as you can, pass other riders, look to take the lead and hold it—an all-out attacking style. Going to Moscow and competing against other top riders, he soon learned that his tactics didn't always work. To put it bluntly, he admitted, "I had no idea what I was doing." He took the lead, and held it for several laps. Suddenly, he found himself running out of gas. This wasn't a time trial in New Mexico or a race around the Richardson Bike Mart. The other riders knew what they were doing, bided their time, and finally passed the tiring Armstrong. Though he finished out of the money, a disappointment to him, he had nevertheless made an impression on others.

U.S. Cycling Federation officials saw tremendous potential in the hot-spirited young rider, while a Russian coach said, flat out, that Lance was the best young rider he had seen in a long time. So there were plenty of positives to take away from Moscow.

Back in Plano, however, there was one big negative. School officials gave Lance an ultimatum. Unless he made up all the work in each subject that he had missed during the six weeks he had been gone, he wouldn't graduate with his class. Lance sucked it up, attended a private academy, made up the work, and graduated with his class.

Finally school days were over and Lance had to make some decisions. College wasn't an option because there was simply no way he could pursue a cycling career at an American college. While trying to decide, he just stayed around Plano for a few months; in the fall, he watched most of his friends go off to various colleges. During this time, however, he was also competing in local bike races and traveling a bit with a sponsored team. In addition, he was competing in 10K runs and triathlons, and beating adults regularly. But he wasn't happy in Plano, especially with his friends gone. As a cyclist, he already knew the place to be was Europe. He did some riding for his old friend, Jim Hoyt, but the two had a falling out when Lance got into a fistfight with another rider. Finally, he knew it was time to leave town.

After his trip to Moscow, Lance had been named to the United States National Cycling Team and finally received a call from the team's new director, Chris Carmichael. Carmichael was well aware that cycling was a go-nowhere sport in the United States and hoped to change that. His objective was to develop a group of exciting young American riders. He had a list of the top kids and Lance was among them.

At the age of eighteen, Lance left Plano, Texas, and didn't look back. He was going head-first into cycling, an all-or-nothing rider whose idea of strategy was to get on the bike and go as hard as he could for as long as he could. It was not the way to win international races. Chris Carmichael knew immediately that there was a great deal to teach this young upstart, a Texan with attitude, but he also saw the great potential in the strong, young rider. He began getting Lance ready for his first big international race, the 1990 amateur World Championships in Utsunomiya, Japan. This was a 115-mile road race, held over a difficult course that included a long climb. On race day, the temperatures went into the nineties, making conditions even more difficult for the riders.

Chris Carmichael laid out the strategy for Lance. He told him he expected him to stay back in the pack for a good part of the race, and to watch for his signal before Lance made a move to the front. He explained that the heat made it imperative for Lance not to take the lead. The lead racer has to deal directly with a headwind, while the riders in the pack can draft behind the lead rider and avoid some of the tiring effects of the wind.

"I don't want to see you near the front catching the wind," Carmichael said, with absolute certainty. "Stay back and wait."

Did Lance listen? Does a wildcat hold back when it sees its prey? He followed instructions for one lap, then decided to test his wings. On the second lap he took the lead and sprinted way out ahead of the field. For the next three laps he pedaled like mad and built a lead of nearly a minute and a half. That's when the heat began to get him. At the halfway mark, Lance was hurting, and about thirty riders had already caught him. The heat and the climbs took their toll and, while Lance didn't quit, he finished the race in eleventh place.

Despite ignoring instructions and wilting in the heat, Lance had still managed the best American showing ever in the race. Chris Carmichael wasn't really angry. He understood Lance's desire to win and the way he preferred to attack a course. It wasn't always the right way, but Carmichael felt that if Lance's talents could be properly channeled, he would not only succeed, but excel. He told Lance again that he felt Lance could have taken a medal if he had conserved his energy and made a late move. Then he added, "I'm convinced you're going to be a world champion, but there is still a lot of work to do."

Much of the work seemed to involve making Lance understand the total nature of the sport. He had to learn strategy and realize that he couldn't always attack, though his instincts told him to do just that. Even though Lance had fared better than any American rider ever in the amateur championships, Chris Carmichael pulled no punches when he told the young rider that the top guys in the world were all as strong or stronger than he was. He explained that it was often tactics that separated riders of equal or near-equal ability. Lance had to listen to those who had been there, and he had to ride. The more experience he got, the better off he would be.

So he raced, spending more than half the year in Europe with mixed results. When he returned to the States he moved to Austin, Texas, where he found a more relaxed atmosphere than in Plano. People weren't as interested in status, or who you were, what you wore, and what you did. Lance enjoyed training there because there were so many bike trails and back roads where he didn't have to battle traffic. He got himself a small house not far from the University of Texas campus. His goal was to race as an amateur through the 1992 summer Olympic Games, which would be held in Barcelona, Spain. Then he would turn professional. Until then, he continued to race for two teams. In the United States, he was part of the Subaru-Montgomery team, while in Europe he rode under the banner of the United States National team.

Besides tactics, Lance had to learn about the politics of cycling. This may sound strange, for in most sports this kind of thing doesn't exist. Good sportsmanship, yes; politics, no. But in cycling, things are different. Lance also learned that while it's an individual who wins a race, the sport is a lot more about *team* than most people think. Within a team of riders, each individual has a particular job because many of the riders are simply not expected to win. The slower riders, for example, are called *domestiques,* or servants, because they do what can be considered the grunt work. They often lead for a time up hills, pulling the faster riders behind them. In other words, they are blocking the wind for their teammates, making the climb easier for them so they can go hard at any time. They also protect the team leader during various danger zones in a stage race. The team leader, obviously, is the cyclist with the best chance to medal or win.

During some races, spectators will see a huge pack of riders moving as if they were one big group. This pack is called the *peloton*. The speed of this large group of riders can vary from around twenty miles per hour to perhaps forty. If there were no unwritten rules within the peloton, a helter-skelter situation might result, with riders bumping, pushing, falling, and perhaps even fighting. In other words, the peloton could easily become a dangerous mess. Instead, riders often help each other in a kind of one-hand-washes-the-other situation. If you help, someone will help you. If you don't, enemies can result. A rider who gets a reputation for being ruthless and reckless within the peloton may soon find himself in trouble, despite the efforts of his teammates. It isn't always easy, but the smart rider will observe a certain etiquette and political correctness within the pack.

These were not easy lessons for someone with Lance's temperament. He always wanted to win so badly that it was difficult for him to give anything, even in the peloton. But he gradually learned that discretion was the better part of valor and, as much as possible, did what was necessary to keep from being labeled a rebel. As was his plan, he rode in the 1992 Olympics as an amateur and finished fourteenth in the Olympic cycling road race. Yet despite the disappointment of not even approaching a medal, Lance's obvious natural talent caught the eye of someone who would help take him to the next level.

The man's name was Jim Ochowicz, who was the director of a professional racing team sponsored by Motorola. The team was made up of mostly American riders, and Ochowicz was constantly on the lookout for new young riders who he felt would improve the team while having a good chance to excel as individuals. After watching the Olympics, Jim Ochowicz made it a point to set up an appointment with Lance.

He told him straight out that his goal was to find an American rider with the ability to win the Tour de France. Only one American, Greg LeMond, had ever won the Tour, and he had done it three times. None of Ochowicz's riders had ever won. When Ochowicz asked Lance about his goals, the answer he got was short and to the point.

"I want to be a professional rider," Lance said, "and I don't want to just be good at it. I want to be the best!"

That was the kind of answer Ochowicz was looking for. He offered Lance his first professional contract. The immediate plan was for Lance to race in Europe with the Motorola team. His first event was the 1992 Classico San

Sebastian, and it would be a rough one. It was a one-day race that covered more than one hundred miles in Spain. The terrain was difficult and the weather often bad. Sure enough, on race day the weather lived up to its reputation: It was raining very hard, and it was cold. That makes it extremely difficult for riders. They can't wear a lot of clothing, so they get cold easily. It's extremely difficult to dress lightly and ride well in bad weather.

The icy rain really affected Lance and he soon found himself at the back of the pack, dropping further and further off the lead. As the race wore on, riders began dropping out, too exhausted to continue to battle the elements. As Lance saw the field moving further and further ahead of him, he thought about dropping out as well. But he simply couldn't do that, not in his first professional race. He didn't want Jim Ochowicz and his new teammates to think he was a quitter. He would finish the race, no matter what.

Finishing was almost as embarrassing as quitting. Lance crossed the finish line dead last in a field of 111 riders. As he finished, he had to endure laughter and some hissing from the spectators standing by the finish line. He would call it the most humiliating and sobering race of his life, to the point where he actually thought about quitting the sport. Self-doubt had crept into his head; maybe he couldn't compete with the big boys, after all. It was his old friend Chris Carmichael who convinced him to stick with it, to use the race as a learning experience. The positive thing that he had to grab onto was that he didn't quit, that he had shown his new teammates that he was tough. Build from there, Carmichael advised him.

That's just what Lance did. Two days after the disaster at San Sebastian he was competing in the Championship of Zurich in Germany. With much to prove to himself, his teammates, and all the other riders on the tour, he went back to the tactics that had always served him well. He attacked the course like the demon; no holding back, no strategy. He just pedaled his tail off and crossed the finish line in second place. What a difference! In the space of two days, he had gone from being a last-place finisher with a ton of self-doubts to a rider standing on the podium and getting a medal for a second-place finish. There were no thoughts of quitting now. In the often ebb-and-flo world of sports, Lance's confidence soared.

3
On to the
Tour de France

It's one thing to tell an American about a largely European sport, its traditions, politics, and rules of etiquette. It's totally another thing to get him to understand and adopt them. In effect, Lance was still an aggressive young rider who grew up with American sports traditions. Right or wrong, he was filled with attitude and approached his sport with an in-your-face philosophy that said, *Attack, ride hard, take no prisoners.* So while he was moving forward as a top cyclist, he was moving backward in the eyes of many European fans and riders.

Lance himself admitted that he would often ride with a chip on his shoulder and, in effect, look for trouble. He would holler at other riders in the peloton, almost ordering them out of the way, not realizing he was going against the team concept. What he didn't realize was that in the tightly packed peloton, other riders could easily keep someone they didn't like from moving up or breaking out when he chose. More and more riders didn't want to see this arrogant Lance Armstrong win a race. Even his Motorola teammates told him to keep his emotions under control, that he was making too many enemies. Fortunately, his teammates pretty much understood him. They slowly convinced him that he had to put some of his natural instincts on hold and adopt the European racing ethic.

In one race, Lance insulted a highly respected, top Italian rider, Moreno Argentin. Again, it was his temper that got the best of him. He was racing in the Trophee Laigueglia in Italy, a tough, one-day race. The heavy favorite was Argentin. During the stretch run, it turned into a two-man race between Lance and Moreno Argentin, with two other riders close behind. Lance, as always, gave it all he had and crossed the finish line first. Argentin was behind him, but just yards from the finish line he hit his brakes, slowing enough to let the other two riders pass him. Then he crossed the finish line fourth.

Argentin was sending a message. By finishing fourth, he wouldn't have to share the medal podium with Lance. It wasn't so much that Lance had won, but that he had disrespected Argentin in his own country and in front of friends and fans. By stopping his bike and finishing fourth, Argentin was showing he had no respect for Lance and was returning the insult in his own way. Ironically, Lance and Moreno Argentin would later become close friends. All it took was some understanding of the need to play by both the written and unwritten rules, and Lance was finally beginning to learn.

Once Lance realized he couldn't go out there on his own and be the rebel with the perpetual chip on his shoulder, he began listening more to other riders, as well as his advisors, Chris Carmichael and Jim Ochowicz. It was even difficult, however, for Lance to adjust to life in Europe. Everything was different—the food, the accommodations, the climate, and the lifestyle. As much as he loved cycling and winning, he was finding that there was a lot more to being a successful professional rider than just jumping on the bike and pedaling. It would take some time, yet slowly but surely it all began falling into place.

The 1993 season was a real breakthrough for him. He would win ten titles that year, as well as finally tasting the kind of money a top cyclist could earn. That summer, Thrift Drugs, a major sponsor of American cycling, offered a one-million-dollar bonus to any rider who could win the Triple Crown of Cycling, which meant all three of the most prestigious races in the United States. When Lance learned of the bonus money, his competitive juices began to flow, but the money wasn't a slam-dunk by any means. All three races were distinctly different. The first was a difficult one-day race in Pittsburgh, Pennsylvania. Next came a six-day stage race in West Virginia. The last race was the United States Pro Championships, a one-day road race of 156 miles through the streets of Philadelphia.

Each race demanded a different riding style. Most riders were stronger at one kind of racing than another. For example, someone who excelled in a one-day road race might struggle to come back day after day in a six-day stage race. A sprinter who could eat up the pack on flat surfaces might well wilt on the steep hills of a climbing stage. Many felt that the Thrift Drugs bonus money was safe. There wasn't a rider good enough to win all three. But they didn't count on the determination of Lance Armstrong.

He won the first race in Pittsburgh, then

surprised a lot of people by winning the stage race in West Virginia. Up to that point, he wasn't considered a stage racer, yet his determination and strength wore the other riders down. Now, with the U.S. Pro Championships looming, the buzz throughout the cycling world was whether Lance could complete the triple play and win the million-dollar bonus. It was the first time he had attracted so much attention, and it was happening in the United States. The final race in Philadelphia would have 120 competitors, each trying not only to win the race, but to knock Lance Armstrong off the pedestal he was climbing. The race received so much publicity that nearly half a million people lined the streets to watch, an incredible turnout for a bicycle race in the United States.

A much smarter racer now, Lance vowed not to get caught in his old trap of going too fast at the beginning and burning himself out. He wanted to be fresh and fit in the final miles so he could handle any challenge that might arise. Listening to his head and not his heart, he paced himself, staying close enough to the front so he could catch the leaders. With about twenty miles remaining, a little alarm clock went off in his head, the one that said, *Attack!*

He made his move on the steepest part of the course standing up on his bike and pedaling.

But it was no ordinary Armstrong attack. He would later say that he felt a new emotion, rage, and when he made his move he also began to scream. The crowd loved it, but his competitors didn't. A few tried to go with him, but just couldn't keep up.

Within an incredibly short amount of time, Lance had opened up a huge lead. It was now apparent that barring an unforeseen catastrophe, he was going to win the race. When he crossed the finish line, he had won the race by the largest margin in its history. He immediately got off his bike and ran to his mother, giving her a huge hug. They both realized now that all the hard work and sacrifice was paying off.

Later that summer he accepted the ultimate challenge. He would compete in the Tour de France for the first time. For a young cyclist, this should have been a daunting proposition, but confidence was something Lance never lacked. Early in the Tour, Lance made news again. He surprised everyone by winning a stage victory, on the 114-mile ride from Chalons-sur-Marne to Verdun. He did it in typical fashion, sprinting away from the others over the final fifty yards. At the age of twenty-one, he had become the youngest rider ever to take a Tour stage. Only this time, the euphoria over winning a stage was short-lived.

For one of the few times in his career, Lance was unable to finish. After the twelfth stage of the race he could continue no longer. He dropped out, finding that he couldn't keep up with the world's top riders in the mountains. There was no shame in what he did. The mountain stages of the Tour de France had humbled many riders over the years. Lance simply wasn't ready for the arduous climbs, both physically and mentally. However, he had come a long way. While not yet a major Tour de France challenger, in the other races he was proving to be one of the best in the world.

He showed that again later in the season. Though he still tended to revert to the old Lance at times and go out so fast that he would burn out, or *bonk*, as they call it in cycling, he was still a threat to win most major races. The World Championships were held in Oslo, Norway, in 1993, a one-day race that featured most of the top cyclists in the world, including Miguel Indurain of Spain, who was fresh off his third straight victory in the Tour de France. On race day, it was raining. Rain probably creates the worst possible conditions for a major road race because the roads become slick and it's easy for riders to lose control and fall.

Once again Lance hoped he would run a smart race and not burn himself out. Maybe the rain helped in that respect because it wouldn't allow him to go all-out at every turn. In fact, he fell twice that afternoon, but fortunately was able to get back on his bike and continue. The race was a lap race held on an 18.4-kilometer course. With fourteen laps left, Lance was riding in the lead pack, as were Indurain and several other top cyclists. Lance felt it was almost time, and on the second-to-last climb of the race he began his attack. In typical Armstrong fashion he leaped out in front, pedaling as if his life depended on it. He continued down the other side, then attacked the final climb. A number of other riders stayed with him and he knew he couldn't let up, not for a second.

On the final descent he had opened a gap. He just hoped he wouldn't fall victim to the slick roads, not now. When the finish line was in sight he knew he had done it. He had won the World Championships, once again the youngest rider ever to do so. At twenty-one, he had become an international star, and with his natural talent augmented by growing experience in all kinds of racing, it appeared that the sky was the limit. A few years later, however, he would look back at that World Championship with a rather different view.

"In retrospect, perhaps I was too successful too soon," he told a reporter. "The rider crowned

World Champion comes under tremendous scrutiny and at the time I probably wasn't prepared. Of course, I really wouldn't change a thing."

At twenty-one, Lance was a full-time professional cyclist. He would now spend about eight months of the year racing on the European circuit, then come home to Austin, Texas, where he would again see the familiar faces of old friends. There were still many times when he was the sole American in the European races, and that was sometimes lonely for him. However, he was no longer the pesky kid that so many European riders resented. He now had friendship and respect from many of the competitors.

Lance's 1994 season wasn't quite as successful as the previous year, but he began 1995 with a victory in the Tour du Pont, the biggest stage race in the United States. He also spent a great deal of time working on his riding technique, trying to find ways to get the maximum effectiveness from his body. That year he met the great Belgian rider, Eddy Merckx, who had won the Tour de France five times between 1969 and 1974. Merckx and Lance became friends, but when Merckx began to evaluate Lance as a rider, he said something that Lance knew he would have to consider.

Merckx told Lance that he certainly had the

ability to win the Tour de France, but that his body type was holding him back. At 180 pounds and with a thick neck and heavily muscled chest, Lance was a big man, too big for a Tour rider. Merckx felt that unless Lance lost some weight, he would always falter in the mountain stages of the Tour. The more weight a rider has to carry up steep inclines and mountain roads, the more difficult it is, no matter how strong he might be. The trick, Merckx said, was for Lance to lose weight without losing strength, and that isn't always easy.

Though Lance was having a good season in 1995, his coaches felt it was important for him to not only compete in the Tour de France, but to finish it. At twenty-three, he still had plenty of time to win it, but it was important for him to get a taste of the entire race and to cross the finish line, no matter what his final standing. The coaches knew he wasn't ready to win and they told him so. His job was to ride all the stages as best he could, to pace himself and not burn out so he couldn't continue. He still had a reputation as a one-day racer, a guy who could muster all his energy and adrenaline, and even his anger, into one day of manic riding. The stage race was a whole different thing, especially the Tour de France.

The 1995 Tour would be a showcase for

Miguel Indurain, who would set a record by winning the race for the fifth straight time. While Indurain occupied the attention of the press and the fans, Lance was toiling in near anonymity, working hard, pacing himself, and learning more and more about competing in the Tour. Then, late in the race, something happened that had a profound effect upon him. One of his Motorola teammates, Fabio Casartelli, who had won a gold medal in the 1992 Olympics, crashed and was killed while making a descent at high speed. It was a chain-reaction crash in which some twenty riders went down.

Most Tour crashes are relatively minor. Riders often get up and continue in the race. In the more severe crashes, the rider might suffer injuries that prevent him from continuing, but deaths are relatively rare. Fabio Casartelli had the misfortune of going down hard, then striking the back of his head on a curb. The news of the accident and Fabio's death hit Lance hard. Not only was he Lance's teammate, but Fabio was a rider with great potential. He was also a husband and the father of a month-old infant. It was a terrible tragedy, both personal and for the world of cycling.

That night, the entire Motorola team met to discuss whether they should continue in the race or not. Lance's first reaction was to abandon the race, but he and his teammates decided to continue. The final decision was made when Fabio's wife came in and asked them to continue, saying her husband would have wanted it that way. The next day they simply rode together as part of the peloton, no one breaking out or attacking. It was a tribute to Fabio, and the team was given a ceremonial stage victory. Lance called it "another long, terrible day—eight hours on the bike, with everybody grieving."

The next day the team again began to race. The day after, the stage was a run into the city of Limoges. Jim Ochowicz told the riders that this was a stage that Fabio wanted especially to win. Hearing that, Lance immediately set a goal for himself. He wanted to win the stage for his fallen teammate. For the first half of the race he rode within the lead pack, close to Indurain, who was wearing the traditional yellow jersey always worn by the overall leader of the race.

With about twenty-five miles left and a downhill section approaching, Lance suddenly attacked as only he can. Pedaling as if his life depended on it, he bolted to a thirty-second lead in no time flat. Because he had attacked so early, probably too early, the other riders were caught by surprise. The element of surprise worked. Lance lengthened his lead and none of the other riders got close. He won the stage by a minute over his nearest competitor and said it was the most meaningful and special victory of his life. He still was far from winning the Tour, but winning the stage race in honor of his fallen teammate gave him a very spiritual feeling.

"I know I rode with a higher purpose that day," he would say.

This time Lance would finish the entire Tour de France. He knew there was still plenty of work to be done before he could win the overall title. The Tour, he felt, was more than just the longest bicycle race in the world. It required a combination of body and mind to be successful. All the training and strength in the world wouldn't help if you weren't ready for it mentally. He wasn't yet, but felt he was approaching that level step by step.

Later in the 1995 season, Lance would win the Classico San Sebastian, the same race he had finished dead last three years earlier when he made his professional debut. And when he returned to the United States, he established the Lance Armstrong Junior Olympic Race Series, which was designed to promote cycling and racing among young American riders. He was now fully immersed in his sport and wanted to see more American kids become involved.

At the outset of the 1996 season Lance was widely considered one of the best overall cyclists in the world, a rider with the potential to be one of the very best. He looked forward to the upcoming year with unbridled optimism. However, fate had something else in store for him. Though he didn't know it then, his world and his life were about to change in a way that neither he nor anyone around him could ever have expected.

4

A Devastating Diagnosis

The 1996 season started off as if it were going to be one of more success as well as the continued growth of Lance's status in the cycling world. Over the winter, however, he began to notice his right testicle had become slightly swollen. His first reaction, not surprising for an athlete, was that he had somehow injured it on the bike. Most athletes live with some kind of pain, often on a daily basis, and tend to pass off a newfound ache as part of the business. Football and hockey players, participating in what are known as collision sports, don't know a single day during their seasons when something doesn't hurt, often quite badly. Basketball players also push their bodies to the limit, running, jumping, banging under the boards. They, too, experience aches, pains, and soreness almost on a daily basis. It's also important to remember that the American ethic has always been to be tough and play through the pain. You don't complain.

Individual sports are really no different. Runners, triathletes, cyclists, even tennis players go so hard, often to exhaustion, that their bodies sometimes break down. Being on a bike all day on varying terrains and in all kinds of weather isn't an easy task. As Lance himself said, everything hurts—back, feet, hands, neck, legs, and butt. So he paid little attention to the swollen testicle and continued to compete. It certainly wasn't affecting his performance. In early spring he won a race called the Flèche-Wallonne in France, another that no American had ever won before, then finished second in the Liege-Bastogne-Liege, which was a 167-mile course that had to be covered in a single day. So he continued to excel in the major races and then returned to the States to defend his title in the Tour du Pont.

Since no rider had ever won it two years in a row, Lance wanted to win the Tour du Pont very badly. Though it wasn't comparable to the Tour du France, the Tour du Pont was still a tough stage race, covering some 1,225 miles over twelve days, with much of it taking place in the mountains of North and South Carolina. Lance won the race and appeared as strong as ever in doing it. But those who knew him might have seen something different this time. Instead of pumping his fists in victory as he usually did, he crossed the finish line and appeared utterly exhausted. He was. He also noticed that his eyes were bloodshot and his face flushed.

Again, a young athlete coming into the prime of his life and career isn't going to think about a serious illness. He just felt he was run down and needed some rest. He was already pointing to a pair of events later in the summer, the Tour de France and then the 1996 Olympic Games at Atlanta, so he continued to train and race, taking five second-place finishes following the Tour du Pont. In fact, he was poised to crack the top five in international cyclist rankings for the first time. There was still no hint of a major problem.

But once Lance began riding in the Tour de France, it took just five days for him to realize he didn't have it. He had ridden in the rain early in the race and came down with a bad case of bronchitis and a sore throat. He was coughing so much and also had so much lower-back pain that he couldn't even get back on his bike.

After five days he dropped out. He told the press, "I couldn't breathe," something he would say that, looking back, should have served as more of a warning.

He went back to Austin, rested, felt recovered, and began working toward the Olympics. He competed in both the time trial and the road race, finishing sixth and twelfth, way below his expectations. Once again, he just didn't feel right. Back in Austin, he found himself sleeping a lot, and felt achy and drowsy much of the time. He was still rationalizing, passing his problems off on the long season. But it just wasn't like Lance to feel this way. In his own mind, he couldn't imagine anything derailing his career now. He had recently signed a huge, two-year contract to ride with a major French team, Cofidis, for $2.5 million. He had a girlfriend that he was crazy about and had built a new home alongside Lake Austin. He seemed to be close to having it all.

Then, a few days past his twenty-fifth birthday, he had a group of friends over to his house before going to a concert. At the concert, he got a terrible headache that just wouldn't leave him, despite his taking some over-the-counter pain medication. Though the headache was gone in the morning, the strange sequence of symptoms should again have told him something was wrong. Several days later, something finally happened that he couldn't ignore. He began coughing up blood. His doctor in Austin was also a good friend and next-door neighbor. He came over immediately. Because Lance had often complained about his sinuses, the doctor thought they might be the cause of the bleeding.

Again Lance relaxed, not imagining there could be a serious problem, but within a week he awoke to find his right testicle incredibly swollen, almost to the size of a baseball. He called his doctor again, and this time the doctor said Lance had to be checked out immediately, without hesitation. He recommended that Lance seek the opinion of a urologist. The urologist didn't like what he saw and recommended a test called an ultrasound. Once that was done, Lance was immediately sent to have a chest X-ray. By that time, a nervous sense of foreboding was beginning to creep over him. He was told to take the X-rays back to the urologist's office. His doctor friend joined him as the urologist looked at the X-rays. When he finally spoke, his words hit Lance like a thunderbolt.

"This is a serious situation," he said. "It looks like testicular cancer with large metastasis to the lungs."

At first, Lance couldn't believe it. He was

twenty-five years old, a world-class athlete, a guy who always took great care of his body. How could he possibly have cancer? The urologist told Lance he had every right to get a second opinion, but added he was confident his diagnosis was correct and that Lance should proceed to step one, having the cancerous testicle removed immediately, as in the next day.

Lance was understandably shocked by the grave diagnosis. He realized he had been sick with a number of symptoms for quite some time. As an athlete, he just didn't want to give into it. He had been trained to overcome adversity, and for a long time viewed his various symptoms as just another bump in the road. What he didn't know at the time was that testicular cancer is the most common form of cancer in men between the ages of twenty and forty, though it's still rather rare. There are only about 7,500 new cases diagnosed annually, with about 90 percent of the cases completely curable. In fact, it is one of the most curable of all cancers if found early. In Lance's case, however, he had ignored his symptoms for months, allowing the original cancer to metastasize, to spread to other parts of his body. That's why his case was so serious.

The morning after the diagnosis, Lance underwent surgery to remove the cancerous testicle. It was then recommended he see Dr. Dudley Youman, a well-known oncologist based in Houston. Lance was told that speed was all-important. Because the cancer had spread, treatment had to begin immediately. His doctors assured him that cancer treatment had improved tremendously and that he could be cured. His immediate reaction was to get on with it, to do whatever it took. In other words, attack, just like he would when he was racing.

Suddenly, Lance wasn't worrying about the next race, about winning the Tour de France or capturing an Olympic medal. He had another battle to fight now and he knew the consequences if he lost. Win or lose, one thing was certain in his mind at that moment: His career as a bicycle racer was over.

Lance's surgery to remove the testicle went well. The next morning, he met with Dr. Youman for the first time. Lance, like most people, knew what chemotherapy often meant—becoming violently ill and very weak, losing all your hair. It was as if the doctors almost had to kill the patient in order to kill the cancer. One way or another, he knew that a real ordeal lay ahead of him. The doctor told Lance he was in the third stage of the disease, the worst, and that the cancer was now spreading rapidly. He would have his first chemo treatment in a week.

To administer the drugs, a Grosjean catheter would be implanted in his chest and would probably remain there for at least three months. Even to a tough-minded athlete like Lance Armstrong, the prospects for the immediate future had to be extremely frightening.

Because he was a world-class athlete, Lance knew he couldn't hide his illness. On October 8, he held a telephone press conference so that the story would be broken correctly and everyone would have it at the same time. His statement said, in part:

> "On Wednesday, October 2, I was diagnosed with testicular cancer . . . A CT-Scan revealed that my condition has spread into my lungs and abdomen. In terms of degrees of the disease, my condition is considered to be advanced and, thus, yesterday, I began my first day of chemotherapy treatment. I will undergo chemotherapy for at least nine weeks and then, depending on how I respond to treatment, may have to undergo more chemotherapy or other procedures to fight this disease.
>
> "I have the utmost faith in all the doctors with whom I am working and

I am determined to fight this disease and to prevail . . . My oncologist, Dr. Dudley J. Youman, was unable to be here today. However, he has told me that the cure rate for testicular cancer in the advanced stage is between 60 percent and 85 percent. Further, if I do beat this disease I have been assured that there is no reason that I cannot make a full and complete recovery.

"For now, I must focus on my treatment. However, I want you all to know that I intend to beat this disease, and further, I intend to ride again as a professional cyclist. I am unable to say today when I will be back in the peloton but hold out hope that I might still participate in the 1997 season."

In many ways, it was a mixed message to those who heard and then read it. Advanced cancer was never an easy foe, and statistics showed that many people had lost the battle. While everyone was pulling for Lance, many probably felt his chances were slim. And virtually no one thought he would ever return to world-class racing. His friends, however, all rallied around him. Led by his mother, they would provide him with endless hours of support throughout his ordeal.

At his press conference, Lance also announced his intention to become a spokesperson for testicular cancer. "Had I been more aware of the symptoms, I believe I would have seen a doctor before my condition had advanced to this stage. I want this to be a positive experience and I want to take this opportunity to help others who might someday suffer from the same circumstance I face today."

Jim Ochowicz, speaking for Motorola, echoed his thoughts. "All the staff and members of the Motorola cycling team extend their full support to Lance and his family, and will be at his side to support him throughout this difficult time," Ochowicz said. "We now know that Lance is facing the biggest battle of his life, but knowing him as we do we feel sure that he will face this new challenge with all the strength and character that has made him one of the top cyclists in the world. Lance's efforts to beat this illness and his desire to bring awareness to this form of cancer to men around the world reflect the courage of this young man to turn his situation into a positive one. We hope that we can help him raise the worldwide understanding about this illness."

So all the support pieces were in place, as well as plans for the day when Lance was once again healthy. In the months that followed, it would sometimes be difficult for Lance to keep his optimistic outlook. The fight he was facing would turn out to be much more difficult than anyone had anticipated.

5
A Profile in Courage

Originally, Lance's chemotherapy was supposed to begin one week after his surgery. But the schedule had to be pushed up when tests showed that Lance's cancer had spread even more in just twenty-four hours. It was a rapid progression that obviously had the doctors worried. With chemo set to begin, it was suggested to Lance that he might consider one other thing. Chemo would make him temporarily sterile, a condition that might not reverse itself. If he recovered but was still sterile, he could never father a child. Before starting his chemo, Lance went to a sperm bank in San Antonio so that a sample of his sperm could be stored for possible future use.

It was all unnatural and unnerving. That done, Lance had to begin his treatment. He was told he would be taking a cocktail of three drugs—bleomycin, etoposide, and cisplatin. Though the names are probably meaningless to the average person, just strange medical terms, cancer patients learn them quickly. The most important of them was cisplatin, made from platinum and developed by Dr. Lawrence Einhorn. It had saved the lives of many testicular cancer patients since its development. Lance was told that had he gotten the disease some twenty years earlier, he would have been dead in six months. Now, it seemed, with the modern drugs, he did have a chance to recover.

Because the treatment was so toxic and could make him feel very sick, it would be administered for one week, then he would have two weeks off so his body could recover and develop more red blood cells. Oddly enough, the first treatment didn't make Lance feel very sick. Because of his nature, sitting still wasn't an option. Feeling good enough, he got up every morning and walked. Then, in the evening, he confounded everyone by going for a ride on his bike. Riding was not only therapy, it gave Lance a sense of normalcy, a sense that he was still somehow in control of his life. Though he was acutely aware of his condition, riding made him feel less like a patient and more like a man who was in a race, this time a race to save his own life.

At first, Lance's body tolerated the chemo very well. He even felt at one point that maybe they weren't giving him enough. At the same time, Lance began to read everything he could find about cancer. He wanted to understand everything that was being done and why. If there were any decisions to be made, he wanted to be educated enough to make them correctly, and not leave everything to others. Then one evening, Lance was opening the mountains of mail he was receiving and found a letter from a Dr. Steven Woolf at Vanderbilt University Medical Center. In the letter, Dr. Woolf urged Lance to explore all treatment options and also suggested strongly that he consult with Dr. Lawrence Einhorn, who had developed the use of cisplatin. Dr. Woolf felt there were treatments that would minimize any side effects that might hamper Lance's ability to race if he were to make a full recovery.

That was something Lance had not considered. Without going into all the medical ramifications and technicalities, Dr. Woolf was concerned about one of the drugs Lance was taking, bleomycin. Apparently, bleomycin had a toxic effect on the liver and lungs. The doctor felt that prolonged use of the drug would permanently affect Lance's lung capacity and thus his ability to race. He felt there were other choices and that Lance should look into them. There were facilities to consider in Houston, New York, and at Indiana University where Dr. Einhorn continued his work.

Lance's decision to seek other opinions almost immediately led to yet another complication, a very frightening one. He faxed his medical records to both Houston and Indianapolis, and there was an almost immediate reply from Houston. After reviewing the records, the oncologists asked why Lance had not yet had an MRI done on his brain. When his mother asked why that would be necessary, she received a shocking reply. The doctors said some of the numbers on his recent tests indicated to them that the cancer might very well have spread to his brain.

Once again Lance underwent a test that was frightening in that the results could be devastating. They were. As soon as the results came back Dr. Youman told him, "You have two spots on your brain."

How could it be any worse? Whenever anyone hears something is in his brain, a myriad of thoughts must go through his head. Is this going to affect my mind, my ability to think, to see, to talk? Am I going to have seizures? Will I be able to recognize my family and friends? Lance undoubtedly went through this whole process. The only positive he made out of it, if you could call it a positive, was that he had now heard all the possible bad news. That done, it was time to fight back.

He knew the odds for recovery were dropping. Not only was the cancer in his lungs, but it had now spread to his brain. At this point, he decided he had to find the place that would give him the best chance for recovery. He told his doctors that he wanted to go to Houston and they told him that was a good idea. Once in Houston, the doctors outlined a program that was at once frightening and something that he would have to consider carefully.

The Houston oncologists said they would continue using the drug bleomycin, the one that could damage his lungs. They also told him his treatment would be so caustic that he would *crawl* out of the room after treatment. The way the doctor described it was, "Every day, I'm going to kill you, and then I'm going to bring you back to life." They admitted the bleomycin would tear up his lungs and that even if he recovered, he would likely never be able to race again. They told him he would be in terrible pain. When he asked why the treatment was going to be so radically harsh, they told him point-blank that his was a worse-case scenario and that what had been described to him was his only chance of survival . . . if he opted to be treated there.

While Lance was still taken aback by what had been described to him, the doctors added that they wanted to begin treatment immediately because each day that he waited, his condition would worsen. Lance and his mother drove around Houston trying to decide what to do. His mother was plainly horrified by the picture that had been painted and what her son would have to endure. Lance, while able to accept the fact that he was terribly ill, had a difficult time dealing with the image of being reduced to a shell of a person who could barely move or walk during treatment. They called the doctors back home to get their opinions and it was suggested they make one more stop: Indianapolis. Go see Dr. Lawrence Einhorn, who had been the pioneer for the successful treatment of testicular cancer, the doctors suggested. One phone call and Lance and his mother were told to come to Indiana University immediately. They learned that the staff there never turns away cases, no matter how bad they might be.

The first doctors to consult with Lance and

his mother were Craig Nichols and Scott Shapiro, who was a neurosurgeon. Lance liked them immediately. Dr. Nichols had already gone over Lance's medical records and was candid and up-front. He was also optimistic, telling Lance that they felt good about his chances of recovery, adding that they had seen even worse cases that had been cured. But the doctor also admitted the brain lesions had complicated things. Chemo couldn't be used for them. The options were radiation or surgery. But just when things seemed as if they couldn't be worse, Dr. Nichols would say something that would give Lance hope. He told him they would set up a course of treatment designed to eventually get him back to his cycling.

Lance just wanted to live. That was obviously his first priority. Dr. Nichols said they certainly wouldn't compromise his chances for a full recovery. But if he did recover there was no reason he couldn't race again, so it was important to alter the drugs to preserve his lungs. The combination of drugs they would use would not include bleomycin. He would be taking a treatment tagged "VIP" for the drugs it included. These drugs were vinblastine, etoposide, isofamide, and cisplatin. The isofamide would cause Lance more nausea and vomiting, and perhaps more immediate discomfort, but it wouldn't damage his lungs.

The doctors also suggested surgery for the brain lesions. Again, they were looking to his recovery. If they used radiation he might be left with a slight loss of balance, which might not bother the average person too much, but could be deadly in a high-speed bicycle race. The doctors also pointed out that the lesions appeared to be on the surface of his brain, which would make the surgery much easier. After hearing everything the doctors had to say, Lance and his mother decided quickly that Indianapolis was where they would stay. He would opt for the treatment Dr. Nichols had described. This was where he would roll the dice and hope for the best.

Step one was the surgery. Dr. Shapiro told Lance that the lesions, while on the surface of the brain, were in difficult locations. One was over the part of the brain that controls the field of vision, the other over the center of coordination. Both these faculties, of course, have to be 100 percent for a racer. Brain surgery is always extremely frightening because any kind of damage to the brain can result in some sort of diminished capacity. The doctor did tell him, however, that if the surgery went well, he would recover from it quickly.

The surgery took six hours. Dr. Shapiro was

able to successfully scrape away the lesions. As with all such procedures, tissue samples were sent immediately to the pathologist, and when Lance awoke he finally received a piece of positive news. The lesions were composed of necrotic tissue. In other words, they were dead cells, which meant they weren't spreading. The doctors weren't sure what had killed the cells, but it was the first stroke of good fortune since Lance's ordeal had begun. Maybe, just maybe, it was a sign of things to come, though the worst still lay ahead.

Now it was time for the serious chemo. Lance described it as "one long IV drip." The side effects were nasty. As he said, when he wasn't in pain, he was vomiting. He lost all the hair on his body. When the chemo was dripping into his veins there was always a burning sensation. He was coughing constantly and spent a great deal of time in the bathroom. This routine, the drugs and the side effects, had taken full control of his life. To a cancer patient undergoing this kind of treatment, it seems like there is nothing else.

Lance underwent four cycles of treatment over three months. The side effects became worse with each cycle because of the buildup of toxins within his body. By the time he had the fourth cycle, he would be spending a great deal of time just laying in a fetal position and retching. It was a terrible ordeal, but the only chance Lance had to get well.

Chemo doesn't just kill cancer cells. It kills healthy cells as well, and also attacks bone marrow, muscles, the linings of the throat and stomach, and even the teeth. The patient is susceptible to many infections, bleeding gums, and loss of appetite. But as difficult as it was, Lance still had the full support of his friends and the unending devotion of his mother. Someone was always there for him, though he sometimes had a strong sense of being alone in his battle. He tried to keep as much control over his life as he could by always monitoring his medications, asking questions, and visualizing the chemo driving the cancer cells from his body. Still, too often, when he was feeling at his worst from the medication, he would feel as if things were slipping away, either because he couldn't stay awake or felt disoriented. The gamut of emotions he experienced must have put him on a roller-coaster which was going up and down between life and death.

The chemo and the tests to monitor its effects continued. Finally, in November, the numbers coming back began to look more favorable, and a short time later Dr. Nichols said the words Lance wanted to hear.

"You're responding to the chemo," he told

Lance. "In fact, you're ahead of schedule."

Each week the readings were better than the last. Finally, the doctors could say it: He was recovering. The telltale number, Lance's HCG level, had dropped all the way to ninety-six. Earlier in November it had been at 92,000. It looked as if Lance was going to make it. In fact, he was almost well. Needless to say, he started to feel optimistic again. In fact, he told one friend that "when [cancer] looked around for a body to hang out in, it made a big mistake when it chose mine."

He was also beginning to think about riding. During chemo, Dr. Nichols didn't want him to stress his body, even when he was home between treatments. He didn't say no riding, but he implied it. But riding still made Lance feel good, even if he just got on the bike for a few minutes, which was about all he could manage. By the time his treatments had ended, he would ride loops around his neighborhood for about thirty minutes or so, but it was difficult. This was not racing. In fact, it was barely riding. But at least he was back on the bike.

Lance's final chemo session was on December 13, 1996. He would soon be going home for good. With the worst hopefully behind him, there were suddenly other considerations. Dr. Nichols, who had always been totally honest with Lance, said that all signs were pointing to a recovery, that he was one of the lucky ones who had cheated cancer. He also had another suggestion. Because of Lance's high profile in the athletic world, Dr. Nichols suggested he become an activist and help encourage others who were battling the disease. Lance saw it that way as well. He was thankful for the doctors and for the dreaded chemo, which despite the ordeal it had put him through, seemed to have done its job and done it well.

Besides talking to and encouraging other cancer patients, Lance would also form the Lance Armstrong Foundation. It began as an international, nonprofit foundation established to benefit cancer research and promote urologic cancer awareness and the importance of early detection. It would later evolve into a world leader in the concept of "cancer survivorship," helping people manage and survive the disease.

Lance had quickly made the transformation from cancer patient to cancer survivor. He knew firsthand that cancer didn't have to be a death sentence, and that was a message he wanted to get across to others. It probably didn't dawn on him then that perhaps the best way to show this to the world was to get on his bike and become a champion again.

6

On the Road
to Recovery

Lance remained in the hospital for just a few days after his final chemo session. Though he appeared to have beaten the disease, his doctors reminded him that he would need monthly tests to make sure there were no traces of the disease in his system. As a rule of thumb, cancer survivors can only consider themselves cured if they remain disease-free for five years. The first year is usually the most crucial. If Lance's cancer was going to return, it would likely happen within twelve months.

So there would still be a little doubt lurking in the back of Lance's mind. As he said, "I wanted to be cured now. I didn't want to wait a year to find out." But once back home, Lance was able to relax more. He played golf with friends and worked on plans for his foundation. He went to Dr. Youman's office in Austin every week for tests, with the results sent to Indianapolis. A few weeks later he got the word that, as of that moment, there wasn't a trace of cancer in his body.

For a cancer patient, even one like Lance who is pronounced cancer-free, there are still issues. The body may be cancer-free, but the mind is always wondering whether it will remain that way. Lance was officially in *remission,* which meant the cancer was gone, but he still had to be checked to make sure it didn't come back. That can prey heavily on the mind, especially in the early months, and Lance often found himself wondering if the cancer would come back, or if it already had. Each time he waited for the results of a test he held his breath. And when he received the news that he continued to be cancer-free, he breathed a huge sigh of relief.

Of course, he couldn't be a cancer survivor and nothing else. He knew that in the coming months he would have to make some big decisions about what to do, if not for the rest of his life, then for the immediate future. Lance was thinking about riding again in the spring of 1997. One of the reasons was financial. The

Cofidis team that he had signed with for $2.5 million had voided his contract when he became ill because he was unable to race. He felt that if he went into training and at least tried to come back, he could lock the sponsors back in to the second year of the contract.

Once again, Lance began to train on the bike. It must have seemed as if he were starting all over again, riding the familiar roads in and around Austin. He would sometimes ride for four hours at a time, covering over a hundred miles. Other days, however, he would be exhausted after just an hour. It was an up and down scenario, good one day, not so good the next. For awhile he felt run down and then caught a cold. Still worrying about cancer, he felt it might be back and quickly went to Dr. Youman. But he was reminded that the chemo had compromised his immune system; because of that, he was susceptible to infection.

When Lance spoke to Dr. Nichols in Indianapolis, the doctor suggested he take it easy and not consider any real training for the rest of the year. His system simply hadn't had the time to recover from the hit it had taken from the chemo. Now there were two things to worry about—a recurrence of the cancer, and whether or not he would ever be a world-class racer again. In a way, it was a Catch-22. Lance was ready to train hard, but he felt if he did train hard, it might trigger a return of his illness. There was a great deal up in the air when it came to his future.

The best thing that happened to Lance that year was meeting Kristen Richards. In fact, he had met her when he announced the formation of his foundation. She was an account executive for an advertising and public-relations firm that was helping to promote the event. At the time, Lance was still seeing a longtime girlfriend, but when they broke up, he began seeing Kristen. Soon the two would become inseparable. Kristen knew Lance's situation, but it didn't seem to bother her a bit. They just hit it off, simple as that.

Since he was no longer training, Lance had time to relax. He and Kristen traveled to Europe and just had fun. Lance realized that he had begun training as a professional athlete before he was twenty years old. This was one of the first times he could just hang out without worrying about his next race or training session. By the end of the summer Lance was looking healthier than he had in some time. His hair was back and his weight was nearly 160 pounds. He was still twenty pounds lighter than he had been as a racer, but he also remembered being told that he would never win the Tour de France at his previous weight. Finally, the new, leaner Lance Armstrong decided he would try to race again. This time he would make a serious effort to come back.

One problem was a sponsor. He and his representative tried to revive their deal with Cofidis, but the company refused. They felt that Lance would never ride at a world-class level again. Apparently, they also felt it would reflect badly on them if Lance were to become ill again while a part of their team. On September 4, 1997, Lance and his reps called a press conference to announce his return to racing for the 1998 season. At the same time, they made it known that he was no longer with Cofidis and would welcome overtures from other teams. None came.

In the fall, Lance approached a relatively new cycling team, one created in 1996 and sponsored by the United States Postal Service. It seemed a strange idea, the U.S. Postal Service sponsoring a competitive cycling team that would race at the international level. One of the reasons the team had been put together was the Tour de France. Because it was an international event watched by millions, it provided the Postal Service with great public relations and advertising benefits.

At first, Lance couldn't come to an agreement with the team. He felt the base salary was too low. Finally, after negotiating a series of incentive clauses into the contract, he signed. He was now a member of an American racing team, the U.S. Postal Service, and he wanted to make them proud. Then, before the year was out, Lance and Kristen Richards became engaged to be married. His life seemed to finally be falling back into place.

On October 2, Lance officially became a cancer survivor. That was the one-year anniversary of his diagnosis. Doctors told him there was now just a minimal chance the disease would return. You can't get much better news than that. Now he could concentrate on returning to competitive racing. Whenever he talked to the press, however, the subject of his illness was almost sure to arise.

During an interview in December of 1997, he was asked point-blank if he worried that the hard work needed to become a world-class racer once again would lower his resistance and possibly cause him to have a relapse.

"Now I don't have those thoughts," Lance said. "After I passed the one-year marker, and my doctors became more optimistic, I became less frightened. My doctors feel as if I can continue as I did before, and so do I."

Lance was also asked why a country as large as the United States hadn't produced more cycling champions. "Our society just doesn't support and reward our potential [cycling] champions," he said. "Our kids are more interested in football, baseball, and basketball."

In answering another question, Lance admitted that he hadn't been totally prepared for his early success, especially winning the World Championships at the age of twenty-one.

"Cycling is a traditional sport and the rider crowned World Champion comes under tremendous scrutiny, and at the time I probably wasn't prepared. But also, I wasn't paying much attention, either. In retrospect, perhaps I was too successful, too soon."

It was apparent that Lance had been doing a great deal of thinking about his early career and his relationship to his sport. Perhaps his reflections were due to the fact that he thought it had all been taken from him. Now, he was on the brink of getting a second chance. It was still way too early to tell if that second chance would be successful. But if it was, there were many indications that Lance would handle things differently this time. Now, it was up to him, and also whether his body would respond to intense training.

In January of 1998, Lance and Kristen moved to Europe with the U.S. Postal team. He began training in earnest. It wasn't easy. There were good days, and days when nothing seemed right. The problem was that Lance was still wary of his illness, and when he didn't feel good on the bike, he began to worry. He worried that the cancer might return, and also that his body had taken too much of a beating with the chemo treatments to simply bounce back. If that was the case, he would never be a world-class cyclist again.

In addition, he wasn't getting any new endorsements. Endorsements are always a big part of a cyclist's income, not to mention an important way to get him out in front of the public. In a way, Lance was a forgotten man, a former top cyclist who almost reached the top but had the misfortune to be struck down by illness. He knew the only way he would reverse his fortunes was to win. He began his comeback in February of 1998 in the Ruta del Sol, a five-day race through Spain. It was his first race in some eighteen months. Lance worked hard but didn't have the old magic. He finished in fourteenth place.

Sure, there were positives. First of all, he had done it. He finished, and he finished ahead of a lot of riders. In addition, he returned to the sport he loved only a year and a half after being made weak, sick, and almost helpless during his rounds of chemo. Yet he found himself depressed after the race, for an old, familiar reason. Simply put, Lance Armstrong was used to winning. He was used to attacking and blowing other riders away with his speed and determination. He also hated all the media attention his first race back had generated. But that goes with the territory. The entire event, with all the emotions involved, probably just overwhelmed him a bit.

Lance said he wished he could have just been another anonymous rider that no one noticed. "I just wanted to ride in the peloton and get my legs back," he said.

Two weeks later he was back on the bike, racing in the Paris-Nice, a difficult, eight-day stage race with a reputation for being run in difficult weather. It may not have been the best choice given the circumstances. Before the race began, there was a time trial that was used to determine which riders would be in the front of the peloton. Lance again gave it all he had and finished nineteenth. While people congratulated him on his showing, he again felt disappointment. His desire to win was the one thing that had not been diminished by his illness.

A day later the first stage of the race began. Not surprisingly, it began in brutal weather, with a cold rain pelting down on the riders and a nasty crosswind making it more difficult to ride. The wind made the rain feel even colder. The weather brought back memories of other difficult days on the bike, but this time it seemed worse. Lance remembered almost using the bad weather to his advantage in the past, continuing to push until the other riders gave in. Not this day. When one of his teammates got a flat, they all stopped. Once they resumed, they were some twenty minutes behind the leaders. All seemed lost already.

Finally, as another gust of wind whipped across his body and almost made him lose control of the bike, Lance lost control of his resolve. He pulled over, stopped, and removed his jersey. He had quit. At the end of the stage, when the entire U.S. Postal team returned to the hotel, they found Lance packing his bags.

"I quit," he told them. "I'm not racing anymore. I'm going home."

Once again he had done something that was considered very "un-Lance-like." Lance Armstrong had never in his life been a quitter. He showed that in his racing and he showed it all over again in his battle against cancer. But racing through the streets of France in the wind and rain had triggered a new emotion. It wasn't so much his performance. He said he felt strong. Suddenly, he just didn't want to be there sitting atop a bike and racing. He said he didn't know anymore whether this was what he wanted to do for the rest of his life.

The conflicting emotions he was experiencing undoubtedly had much to do with his illness. It's not likely that anyone who endured what Lance did could have the same priorities, the same values, the same aspirations as they did before. Advanced cancer, the constant thought that you might not make it, and even your ultimate recovery has to change you. Realistically, it was probably too much to expect Lance to just resume racing with the same singlemindedness he had shown before. It wasn't as if he had recovered from a broken leg. He had recovered from an advanced case of testicular cancer from which he originally had a "coin-flip" chance of making it. That in itself could qualify as a miracle.

At the Paris-Nice race, all these things and more were going through his mind. Besides his recovery, he was engaged to a woman he wanted to marry. His health was once again good, but in the back of his mind he still feared the possibility of relapse. It's not surprising that while riding a bicycle through the cold, rainy, windy streets of France, it all seemed suddenly insignificant, a place he simply did not want to be. Though he was fit, he couldn't have expected to win right away. That probably wasn't the problem. It was simply of matter of rethinking priorities. He just found he didn't have a passion for racing anymore.

"I don't know how much time I have left," he would tell Kristen, "but I don't want to spend it cycling."

Back in Austin, Lance admitted to his friends and advisors that he simply didn't love racing anymore. Because it's such a demanding sport, riders *must* love it. He also said that because his illness had turned his life upside-down, nothing was the same. What he had to do was find himself all over again. If it turned out that racing was what he wanted, then he could go back. If not, he was done and there would have to be something else.

What Lance might have overlooked was the fact that he had always been an athlete, a competitor. That had been his mindset since he was a teenager, and it would be a difficult mindset to lose, especially at the age of twenty-six. But once home, Lance began to play a lot of golf and hang out with old friends. Finally, Kristen, Chris Carmichael, Jim Ochowicz, and other members of Lance's support team told him it was too early to announce his retirement. Why not ride, they suggested, in the U.S. Pro Championships in

Philadelphia in May? Then, if he still wanted to call it quits, he could announce it after racing one last time in the United States. Lance thought about it and agreed.

7

A Comeback
Begins in Earnest

It was time for some serious training, but in an environment of Lance's choice, one in which he felt he could thoroughly enjoy himself. He decided to go to Boone, North Carolina, in the Appalachian Mountains. Lance liked the area, and it brought back good memories because it was on the route of the Tour De Pont, a race Lance had won twice. Chris Carmichael was there, as was a former teammate from Motorola, Bob Roll, who would ride with him. Lance would almost be starting over. The hiatus in Austin had seen him gain a few pounds and lose some muscle tone. He was already out of shape.

It was old-fashioned training, the way it

used to be—no crowds, no frills, just riding and more riding. Lance went out every day and rode in all kinds of weather. The experience brought Lance back to earlier days and he began to just enjoy the act of riding hard, of feeling his body tire, of working against the elements and pressing on. In the evenings the men ate and talked and laughed about old times, all the things that had brought Lance so close to the pinnacle of his sport before his illness had struck. Going to North Carolina was almost like going back in time, when things were much simpler, when Lance would get on his bike and attack, just one man against everyone else.

The real turning point came when the group decided to ride up Beech Mountain, which was a five-thousand-foot climb and part of the Tour Du Pont. Lance rode the mountain as if he were again racing in the Tour. He left Bob Roll in his wake and continued to drive hard, thinking of his many victories and the satisfaction he had always gotten from riding. When he finally reached the top, Chris Carmichael pulled up behind him in his car, ready to load Lance's bike on top for the drive down.

"Nope," Lance said. "I'm riding down."

Once again Lance Armstrong realized how

much he loved being on a bike, how much he loved competing, against both himself and others. He felt his life was once again beginning to fit together and he now made plans for another comeback, one he wouldn't abandon. In May, he further solidified his life by marrying Kristen Richards in Santa Barbara, California. There was no real honeymoon, because Lance didn't want to take time away from his bike. This time he was intent on trying to regain his former status in the cycling world, and if he could do that, to go beyond it.

He was ready in time for the target race, the U.S. Pro Championships. This time he was far from embarrassed. He rode a strong race and finished fourth. Even though he didn't win, he felt good about his effort and had no doubts about continuing his comeback. The next logical step was a return to Europe to compete against the best. Lance and Kristen moved to Nice, France, and he continued to compete in select races. He began with the four-day Tour of Luxembourg and surprised a lot of people by winning. It was the first victory of his comeback and, he said, erased the last vestiges of self-doubt that he might have had about racing. Now, he knew he could win again.

He still wasn't ready to win them all. He finished fourth in the week-long Tour of

Holland, then made the decision to skip the 1998 Tour de France. He felt he wasn't ready for the rigors of a three-week stage race, especially the biggest in the world. But by September he felt he was ready for bigger fish and entered the Tour of Spain, called the *Vuelta a Espana*. It was similar to the Tour de France in that it was a three-week stage race of more than 2,300 miles. Not only did Lance finish, but he finished fourth, just missing a third-place medal by six seconds and riding only two minutes and eighteen seconds behind the winner. This wasn't just a big step in his comeback; it was monumental.

Up to this point, Lance's reputation had been based mostly on his ability to win one-day races, to dig down deep and outsprint his competitors to the finish line. Because of his track record before his illness, he was never considered a threat in the longer stage races, especially those the length of the Tour de France. Now, he had come in fourth in the Vuelta. Not only had he served notice to everyone else in the cycling world that a new stage-race force was on the scene, but he realized something about himself, something just a short time earlier he never thought possible.

"Not only was I back," he said, "I was better. I felt I was now capable of winning any race in the world."

After finishing fourth in the World Championships in Holland, a race run in brutal weather conditions where only sixty-six of 152 competitors managed to finish at all, Lance knew he was ready for bigger and better things. He returned home to more good news. His cancer foundation was receiving its first two grants for cancer research, which totaled more than three hundred thousand dollars. These gifts were a direct result of monies raised from the 1997 and 1998 Ride for the Roses weekends.

That winter, there was another milestone for Lance and Kristen. They decided they would like to have a child. Because he was infertile from the chemo, the only way they could do it was to use the sperm he had stored before being treated for cancer. Kristen had to undergo in-vitro fertilization, a process that would use Lance's sperm to fertilize her egg. The process was successful, and nine months later Luke David Armstrong was born. It was something everyone who knew Lance and Kristen called yet another miracle.

Though the 1998 cycling season had to be considered a great success for Lance, there was one big trophy that was noticeably missing. He was reminded of it when he received a congratulatory telegram on finishing fourth in the

Tour of Spain from Johan Bruyneel, the U.S. Postal team director. In it, Bruyneel told Lance that he would "look great on the podium at the Tour de France next year."

The message kind of took Lance by surprise. Then he began to think more seriously about it. His recent strong finish in the Tour of Spain had certainly changed his thoughts about stage racing. Now the self-doubts were gone, both about his ability to come back and about his health. Slowly a new and ambitious goal began seeping into his mind. He decided that he wanted to win the Tour de France!

The Tour de France is not only the granddaddy of all European stage races, it is by far the most difficult and demanding. The first Tour was held way back in 1903, when a French newspaper issued a challenge to all riders of bicycles. There were some sixty riders in that first race, with twenty-one of them able to finish a race that was not as long or demanding as it is today. But it must also be remembered that the bicycles were nothing like the high-tech, lightweight racing machines made today. At any rate, with upwards of one hundred thousand people lining the course during that first race, the Tour quickly became a tradition that was there to stay.

Mountain stages were included in the race for the first time in 1910 because the bikes now had brakes capable of slowing and stopping the riders during the steep downhill descents. The bikes in those days had just two gears and the brakes were operated by the feet. Today, the race has evolved into a marvel of modern high technology. The bikes are light enough to lift with one hand, while the riders can be equipped with computers, heart monitors, and two-way radios. But that doesn't stop the race from being a more than two-thousand-mile trek through the Alps and Pyrenees mountains, along narrow roads with steep falloffs, and finally through the streets of Paris. It is a race of attrition, with riders punishing themselves for three weeks with little rest. If you're exhausted at the end of one stage, you had better find a way to be fresh for the next stage the following morning.

Riders who win the Tour de France become instant heroes in their home countries. To the Europeans, the Tour is every bit the equivalent of their other showcase sporting event, the World Cup of soccer. But that only happens every four years. It's also every bit as big as the American Super Bowl or World Series. Those who manage multiple wins become heroes not only in their home countries, but all over Europe. The record is five, shared by Jacques

Anquetil of France, Eddy Merckx of Belgium, Bernard Hinault of France, and Miguel Indurain of Spain. Indurain is the only rider who has won his five races in succession.

Prior to 1999 only one American rider had ever won the Tour. Greg LeMond won the race in 1986 and again in 1989 and 1990. LeMond's story was also dramatic, since after his 1986 victory he was shot and seriously wounded in a hunting accident. Three years later he was back to win another pair of Tours and to solidify his reputation as America's greatest stage racer. LeMond was one of three riders who had won the Tour three times, and eleven riders had won it twice, the earliest being Lucien Petit-Breton of France way back in 1907 and 1908.

The Tour's long and glorious history wasn't always untarnished. Even in the very first race in 1903, some riders resorted to tactics that were decidedly less than reflective of good sportsmanship. They would actually throw tacks and broken bottles onto the roads to try to stop the riders behind them. Drinks were sometimes spiked to make riders sick. Over the years, some competitors have continued to try to think of ways to take unfair advantage of the rest of the field. In recent years, the biggest worry has been athletes who use performance-enhancing drugs. There is testing, but some athletes always try to get around it. That's because the Tour remains cycling's biggest event. It's held during the hottest part of the summer, so the athletes have to be in extraordinary physical condition, especially in the mountain stages.

Prior to his illness, the mountains were always a huge stumbling block for Lance. He was told that at 180 pounds, he was too heavy. Since his illness, however, his body had changed. He was now a sinewy 160, still muscular and strong, but a lot less bulky. That, in itself, augured well for his next foray into the mountains. He had already proved his mettle in the Tour of Spain. Now, it was just a matter of pointing his season toward the Tour de France and hopefully peaking physically at just the right time.

Though the course is never exactly the same, all the riders know what to expect: the biggest test of the year and the race of their lives, no matter how many times they enter. What made Lance's quest more meaningful was the fact that no American team had ever produced a tour winner. When Greg LeMond won his three races, he was a member of a French racing team.

Ironically, while Lance was pointing toward a July date in Paris, he opened the 1999 season in terrible form. There was a crash in the second race of the year that resulted in a shoulder injury that necessitated a couple of weeks off his bike. He was sideswiped by a car in France while on a training run, then had mediocre finishes in the Paris-Nice and Milan-San Remo races. He just wasn't in good form and needed some remedial work on his technique.

Also ironically, Lance noted that now that he was pointing toward winning the Tour de France, he wasn't as effective in the one-day races. He said he didn't have the anger and intensity that always drove him before his illness. But while he might not have been seen by his peers as the overly aggressive rider he had once been, he had developed a single-minded purpose in his riding, and that was to win the Tour de France. For a rider like Lance, who relied so much on emotion, the one-day races suddenly ceased to have the same importance to him. They were more like training for the Tour de France. In fact, Lance said he was willing to sacrifice his entire season to be better prepared for the Tour.

The fact that he was skipping races raised a lot of eyebrows among riders and journalists. Many began to question him about it. Lance didn't mask his intentions.

"I'm putting all my focus into winning the

Tour," he would tell them, in a half-dozen different ways. "All my training and racing decisions are based on that one event."

The entire U.S. Postal Service team had rallied around Lance and was equally committed to helping him win. Though cycling, by its very definition, is an individual sport, in major stage races the entire team is very important to the lead rider. As mentioned earlier, they protect him in the peloton, draft for him to cut down on the wind, and pace him during certain portions of the race. So while it is always an individual who gets the glory for winning the Tour, his team always plays a major role in the winning effort.

At the end of April, Lance entered a one-day race called the Amstel Gold Race. Though he hadn't been focusing on one-day races during the 1999 season, he felt very strong on this day and decided this was one he really wanted to win. Lance was riding at the head of the pack with Holland's Michael Boogerd. With ten miles remaining, Lance continued to lead with Boogerd, also a world-class rider, staying with him. In the final sprint, the point of a race where Lance was rarely caught, Boogerd managed a final push and beat Lance by less than the width of a tire, an incredibly close finish. Lance took the loss hard, as he had in the past.

In addition, because Michael Boogerd was one of the early favorites to possibly win the Tour de France, his loss had a little more bite to it.

Lance returned to his intense, arduous training. He trained in all kinds of weather conditions, on days when no one else would go out, and usually did even more work than he had planned. He was willing to push and punish himself to achieve his goal, which had now almost become an obsession. This was a race the old Lance was told he would never win. And, indeed, before his illness he never thought he could. Now, however, things were different. He knew he had the ability and the heart to win. It was just a matter of putting in the work and then being ready for the biggest three-week push of his life.

By July, Lance felt he was ready. In France, however, he wasn't considered one of the favorites. Maybe there was something of the old feeling that an American team just couldn't cut it in the Tour. The Europeans were simply too experienced. Heck, the experts said, even Greg LeMond had to be part of a European team to win the Tour. Some of the names being thrown around as potential winners were the aforementioned Michael Boogerd, world champion Abraham Olano, Alexander Zulle of Switzerland, and Fernando Escartin of Spain.

Then, a short time before the race was to begin, a reporter asked the legendary champion Miguel Indurain which rider he thought had a good chance of winning. Indurain looked at the reporter and then gave a one-word answer.

"Armstrong!"

8

The 1999
Tour de France

Before the first stage of the Tour there is a short time trial called the Prologue. In 1999 it was held on July 3. It is used to determine where the riders begin in stage one, a kind of seeding system. It is also the first opportunity for the riders to establish themselves to some degree. Because the Prologue is only about eight kilometers long, the riders have to sprint all-out from beginning to end. Even if they let up for just a few seconds, it can cost them dearly at the end. Before the 1999 Prologue, the record for the sprint was 8:12, set by the great Indurain.

The riders started one at a time, as they do in all time trials. The starts were staggered, three minutes apart. That way, there were no head-to-head strategies involved, just a mad-dash sprint with the rider and his bike. On this July day, conditions were good and so were the times. First Olano broke the course record with a time of 8:11. Then, minutes later, Alexander Zulle did even better, crossing the finish line in 8:07. One of Lance's U.S. Postal teammates rode before him and experimented with the gears going up the one hill on the course. That is one way teammates can help each other. The experiment cost him time, but he was able to give Lance some solid advice just before he began.

Finally, Lance took off, riding hard and concentrating on one thing—getting to the finish line as fast as he possibly could. His form was perfect as he sped through the streets, then charged up the hill. He still felt good when he crossed the finish line. He looked up at the clock. When he saw 8:02, he could barely believe it. Then it was confirmed. He had set a new record, beating the record Zulle had set just minutes before by five full seconds and smashing Indurain's old mark by an amazing ten seconds. What was more important was that he would get to wear the fabled yellow jersey, emblematic of being in the lead of the Tour de France. He said the feeling of putting on that jersey was utterly amazing.

Of course, the real race hadn't yet begun. Lance knew it was much more important to be wearing that yellow jersey at the end of the final stage. After the time trial there was one more sweet moment. Lance found himself walking past members of the Cofidis team and their organization. They were the ones who had turned their backs on him when he was so ill and even when he had recovered, didn't think he would ride at a world-class level again. Wearing the yellow jersey after his victory in the time trial, Lance walked by them and couldn't resist.

"That was for you," he told them, with a smile.

But there was still a very long way to go. The race in modern times is a little bit more than rider and bike against the elements. Two cars and a van usually follow each team. The coach can direct his riders through two-way radios. There are earpieces in each helmet and a radio cord wired to a heart monitor so the coach and trainers can watch how the racers are reacting to the various kinds of stress at different stages of the race. In addition, there are spare bikes on top of the vans, a mechanic available if a rider gets a flat, and water and food that can be handed to the riders as they go.

The opening stages of the race always

favored the sprinters, as these stages took place on flat roads across flat countryside. Here, the two hundred or so riders would play a chess game of positioning, the teams trying to help their lead rider. Everyone would be thinking about strategies that would give them an advantage as the race wore on and neared the telltale mountain stages.

The rest of the U.S. Postal riders were there to protect Lance. In the peloton they surrounded him, shielding him from other riders and potential crashes and drafting in front so he had minimal wind. There was one massive crash, but fortunately it happened behind Lance. Still in the early stages, a couple of the favorites, Boogerd and Zulle, began falling behind. Big deficits are difficult to make up—it began to appear it wasn't their year.

Lance just wanted to stay near the leaders. He had to give up the yellow jersey after several stages, but that didn't matter. He just wanted to be in striking distance of the leaders when the race went into the mountains. His strategy included an all-out effort at the time trial in Metz, the final leg before the mountain stages began. An Italian rider named Mario Cippolini tied a Tour record by winning four straight stages and taking over the yellow jersey. The other challengers weren't concerned, though.

Everyone knew Cippolini always faltered in the mountains and because of that, simply wasn't a threat for the overall title. That's the kind of strategy that's used. A rider gets almost a week of glory by winning four straight stages, but none of the other riders really care. They are too busy watching each other.

The time trial at Metz was unlike the opening Prologue. This was a longer run of some fifty-six kilometers; the riders would have to go hard for more than an hour. It was a real test of their endurance and determination. It was also a chance to pick up valuable time in the overall race. It was a course that favored the strong riders, and in the early going, Alexander Zulle had the best time, coming in with a time just over one hour and nine minutes. This time the riders were going off in two-minute intervals.

Abraham Olano was the favorite in this particular stage. He started directly ahead of Lance. As Lance was waiting in the start area, the word came back that Olano had crashed on a curve and lost maybe thirty seconds. He was back on his bike, but it would be difficult to make up the time. That's how quickly fortunes can change in the Tour. One slip, one crash, one flat tire, and the rider loses seconds, maybe minutes. If the crash is bad enough, he might have to drop out of the race.

Lance went out fast, working hard as always and attacking the course. He was flying, maybe too fast. By the third checkpoint his time was a full minute and forty seconds ahead of Zulle. He even caught and passed Olano, something that doesn't usually happen in a time trial. Then, a short time later, he passed another rider who had started a full six minutes ahead of him. But Lance had, indeed, gone out too hard. He started to pay the price in the final portion of the race. His legs began feeling heavy, almost as if they wouldn't move. There was also a headwind and no one to draft. He began to feel he was losing precious time, and wished he had paced himself better.

When he crossed the finish line he was almost afraid to look at the clock. When he did, it read 1:08:36. He had won the stage and beaten Zulle by fifty-eight seconds! Though he was exhausted and concerned he might not recover in time for the next stage, he had regained the overall lead. As he put the yellow jersey on once more, he felt good, very good. Though the race was barely half over, he felt he was in a great position to win and decided he wanted that jersey remaining with him until he crossed the finish line.

Now the Tour was ready to move into the mountains. Lance held a lead of 2:20 over his nearest competitor. But that would mean nothing if he fell apart in the mountain stages. On those steep hills, leads could evaporate as fast as boiling water. This is where the old Lance Armstrong had faltered early in his career. It was the reason he wasn't considered a major threat in stage races. But this Lance Armstrong was different. He already had the lead. Now, if he could control the race in the mountains, he would definitely have a good chance of winning.

Strategy now became even more important. It didn't matter if a rider who wasn't really in contention won a stage. Lance's job was to stay ahead of those who were closest to him and try to increase his overall advantage. In other words, if a rider who was twelve minutes behind him beat him by four minutes in a mountain stage, it wouldn't really matter, if at the same time Lance finished two minutes faster than his closest rivals. Lance would still be increasing his overall lead as well as his chances to win the race.

While all this was happening, word began trickling back to the United States. Normally there was very little interest in the Tour de France in America. There wasn't even much hoopla when Greg LeMond won the race three times. But Lance's story was special. People just couldn't believe that a man who was literally at death's door less than three years earlier was now threatening to win arguably the most demanding and grueling sports event in the world. His agent, Bill Stapleton, expressed the thought that was being highlighted in most of the stories in the American press.

"This guy was on his death bed, and we were more worried about having him live than having him race again," Stapleton said.

Reporters and journalists who normally didn't even cover sporting events were now digging deeper into the story, looking for people to talk about Lance, his battle with cancer, and his amazing comeback. One of his oncology nurses, Janice Thompson, told reporters that it was Lance's fierce determination that helped him in his fight against cancer.

"He had a 'can do' attitude from day one," she said. "He was going to beat this disease; it wasn't going to get him. He's beaten the ultimate competitor—he's beaten cancer. Now I'm sure nothing or no one can intimidate him. He's living large."

And he was riding large, as well. The first mountain stage was a 132.7-kilometer ride that ended in the town of Sestriere. Two of Lance's teammates were climbing specialists and would help draft for him. The two riders that Lance and his teammates would watch would be Alexander Zulle and Fernando Escartin. They were closest to him in overall time. Riders often like to break away on the climbs. Since some are not even in contention, it's the job of the leaders and their teammates to know who to chase and who to let go. The stage featured three major climbs and could be a killer to a lot of riders. For poor climbers, this was where the race would effectively end.

The final ascent of the stage was a long and difficult thirty-kilometer climb to Sestriere and the finish line. The riders had already been pedaling for more than five and a half hours. Add almost constant climbing to that time and it becomes a nearly inhuman task. From this point on it became a matter of will, of who wanted it the most. With just eight kilometers left, Lance was some thirty-two seconds behind the leaders, riding in a second group of five riders, all exceptional climbers. That's when Lance made his move, jumping out in front of the second pack and opening up some distance. He felt strong, like there was more gas in the tank. He continued to work hard as he moved up on the leaders.

Suddenly, Lance was just eleven seconds behind the two leaders and still moving up. When he pulled alongside them they didn't react, so he surged again, taking the lead and opening a slight gap. Still no response from the other two. He accelerated once more, in total control. It's a situation every rider loves to be in, making a move to the front and the other riders not responding. It's a real feeling of power, that you can do it and they can't. When Lance was told that Alexander Zulle was chasing him, he worked even harder, driving toward the finish, not letting up for a second. As he crossed the line he thrust both fists into the air.

What Lance had just done was basically to destroy the rest of the field mentally. He not only proved he could now climb with the best of them, maybe better than the best of them, but he also had won another stage. What's more, he had opened up a gap of six minutes and three seconds over the rest of the field. With that kind of lead, Lance was looking so strong and in such a commanding position that it seemed he would now just have to maintain a consistent pace to win the Tour. Of course, there was always a chance of a crash, illness, or some kind of physical breakdown. But up to this point there were no signs of anything but continued success.

In the next mountain stage, Lance didn't win. He finished fifth. But in doing so, he managed to continue to increase his lead, since the four riders who finished in front of him weren't challengers. Those right behind him, Olano and Zulle, fell farther back. He now had a lead of 7:42 over Olano and 7:47 over Zulle. But just when it seemed only a formality for Lance to finish the Tour at the top, a new controversy arose.

As was the case with other sports in the late 1990s, there were always athletes looking for an edge. One of the ways some athletes tried to do this was to use illegal substances tagged generically as "performance-enhancing drugs," which include but are not limited to muscle-building anabolic steroids. There is a list of banned substances, and athletes in some sports are randomly tested to make sure none of these substances are in their system. The Tour de France, with its status and prestige, has often been a magnet for athletes looking for an edge. Then along came Lance Armstrong, a cancer survivor who was close to death just three years earlier. There was no legal way, many reasoned, that this guy could be blowing away the field in the Tour de France. After all, before his illness he was never remotely a threat to win the Tour, even with all the other titles he had taken. Rumors that Lance was on something began to spread, with some help from the French press.

The most ridiculous allegation was that the

drugs used to battle Lance's cancer had somehow enhanced his ability to race. That was a total joke. Chemotherapy is one of the most debilitating combinations of drugs in the medical world. The drugs weaken and sicken a patient long before they cure him. Had anyone making those accusations seen Lance during his chemo treatments and the aftermath, they would have known how silly they were being. But some found it hard to believe that this man who had been so sick was winning the Tour de France with relative ease. There must be some kind of explanation, people reasoned. It just didn't make sense.

But the drug tests proved that it did. Every one came up negative. Lance didn't like the idea of having blood drawn after nearly every stage, but he couldn't avoid it. They were supposed to be random tests, but he seemed to be the one U.S. Postal Service team rider they always picked to be tested. All the tests showed, however, was that Lance was clean. There were no illegal substances in his system.

"My life and my illness and my career are open," Lance told the press, also citing again that all his drug tests were negative. Yet some members of the French press continued to raise the issue and Lance was forced to stop talking to them for awhile. There was still plenty of racing left and he didn't want any distractions. Because he was the leader, other teams and other riders would try to break him, often by attacking early in a stage and trying to force him to alter his strategy. But Lance and his teammates, for the most part, held true to form. Once, he made an ill-advised charge after the lead pack, but when his coaches told him he was making a mistake, he listened and dropped back. The old Lance might have just continued to attack.

As Lance continued to hold a firm lead on the field, the allegations of drug use continued, despite the negative tests. Finally, he decided to hold a press conference and try to put the allegations to rest, once and for all.

"I have been on my deathbed," he told reporters, "and I am not stupid. I can emphatically say I am not on drugs. I thought a rider with my history and my health situation wouldn't be such a surprise. I'm not a new rider. I know there's been looking, and prying, and digging, but you're not going to find anything. There's nothing to find . . . and once everyone has done their due diligence and realizes they need to be professional and can't print a lot of crap, they'll realize they're dealing with a clean guy."

If nothing else, logic should have told

everyone that a rider who had experienced the horror of chemotherapy would simply not put any substance into his body that had even a remote chance of doing damage or harming him. Yet the speculation continued as he continued to lead the race. There were just so many people who couldn't believe what they were seeing. They just didn't think it was possible.

After the sixteenth stage the riders were finally out of the mountains and Lance still had a lead of 6:15 over Escartin and 7:28 over Zulle. Yet he had to endure another two-hour press conference, one once again dominated by questions about drugs. He began to feel as if the press wanted to break him mentally because none of the other riders could do it. That same day, the International Cycling Federation released the results of all his drug tests so everyone could see everything had come up clean. It was only then that Lance received a glowing testimonial from Jean-Marie Leblanc, the organizer of the race. Fed up from watching what Lance had to endure from the press, Leblanc said, "Armstrong beating his illness is a sign that the Tour can beat its own illness."

The nineteenth stage of the race was another time trial. Lance had such a big lead that his advisors told him to take it easy, not to take any chances, and simply to maintain his position. They didn't want him to risk the one thing that could keep him from winning, a major crash. Lance listened, then shook his head. No way was he going to play safe. He said he was going out hard and was planning to kick butt.

"I'm going to put my signature on this Tour," he said.

With that, Lance went out and gave it all he had once more. Even though he had pretty much wrapped up the overall victory, the other riders didn't want to hand another stage to him. So they all pushed. But when the dust cleared, Lance had won the time trial by a scant nine seconds. With that victory, he became only the fourth rider in the history of the Tour to win all three time trials in one race. The other three were among the greatest ever—Hinault, Merckx, and Indurain. Lance had not only put his signature on the Tour, but on Tour history, as well. Now he just had to ride through the largely ceremonial final stage to make it all official.

At this point, the excitement was also building in the United States. Again, it wasn't so much that an American was on the brink of winning the Tour de France. No, it was the bigger picture, the so-called "feel-good" part of the story, that a cancer survivor was making this miraculous comeback and was on the brink of winning the Tour de France. American journalists were flying to France, while the word came that all the prime-time talk shows in the United States were already scrambling to book Lance once the Tour ended. It's a tradition that the Tour winner travels around Europe and participates in a series of races simply to show off the yellow jersey. Lance felt that was important to him. His agent, however, wanted him to fly to the United States, even if it was just for a day.

But there was one more piece of business to finish. The final stage of the race was an 89.2-mile ride from Arpajon to Paris. Because the race was all but over, the peloton would ride at a relaxed pace until the Eiffel Tower came into view. Then, when the group reached the Arc de Triomphe, the U.S. Postal team would ride in front of the peloton down the Champs-Elysées. Finally, a sprint would take place for ten laps around a course in the center of the city. After that, there would be a final victory lap. It was a longtime tradition for a race that was nearly one hundred years old.

Lance even did interviews from his bike during the ride. When the peloton finally neared Paris, he could feel the emotion building. It further warmed his heart when someone held up a large cardboard sign that said simply TEXAS.

Because there was absolutely no chance of anyone catching Lance, the final ten-lap sprint wasn't highly competitive; Lance was simply careful to avoid any kind of unexpected crash. Finally, as he rode his bike across the finish line, it all sunk in. He had done it. He had come all the way back to win the Tour de France.

Lance was swept up in a myriad of emotions as he stood on the podium for the trophy presentation. His family was there, as were many old friends from Texas. Once the presentation was complete, he leaped off the podium, ran to his wife and hugged her. Then he sought out his mother and hugged her. When a reporter asked his mother if she thought he had bucked the odds to win, she said, "Lance's whole life has been against all odds."

Then Lance and his team got back on their bikes and rode a ceremonial victory lap along the Champs-Elysées. It was a moment for all of them to savor, for each and every member of the U.S. Postal team had played a major role in his victory. When he returned to the press area to answer questions, he told everyone there just how he felt.

"I'm really in shock," he said several times, then added, "I would just like to say one thing. If you ever get a second chance in life for something, you've got to go all the way."

9

A Champion Doesn't Quit

It's virtually impossible to imagine the elation Lance must have felt, the confluence of emotions in winning the Tour de France. To simply say his life had come full circle was an understatement. It would be extremely difficult in the entire annals of sport to find a story as dramatic and fulfilling. As close as his support group had been, including his wife and mother, only Lance could possibly comprehend the full meaning of what he had done. Yet he wasn't going to hog the glory. He made sure that everyone knew he couldn't have won the race without the selflessness of the entire U.S. Postal Service team.

Lance took the advice of Bill Stapleton, his

agent, and flew from Holland to the United States for one whirlwind of a day. Reporters from all over the country had come to New York for just a precious few minutes with him. He began his day by appearing on *CBS This Morning* at five forty-five A.M. and ending it with *The Late Show with David Letterman* at nine P.M. In between, there was barely time for him to get his breath. He went to Wall Street to ring the opening bell at the New York Stock Exchange, then returned for a series of interviews. At one point a producer from NY1 in New York was still signing off as another reporter from KTBC in Austin began asking questions. At the same time, a producer from KCBS Sports Central in Los Angeles was setting up so he could be ready for his station's eight minutes with Lance.

Diana Nyad from *Fox Sports News* waited her turn, as did Jim Rome of *The Last Word*, and many others. It was like an assembly-line of interviews, with Lance essentially telling the same story over and over again.

"I feel almost guilty doing this to him," said Mike Leventhal, a producer for the Bader TV News, where Lance sat for all the interviews. "I usually space things out, give somebody a rest between interviews, but with Lance there just isn't time, just thirty seconds or so to get a drink of water and on to the next."

For Lance, the message he had to send was important, and that was one of the main reasons he had made this overnight trip halfway around the world.

"If I can save five lives by going on some show, it's worth it," he said. "If I can save one life by going on all the shows, it's worth it. I'm prouder of being a cancer survivor than I am of winning the Tour de France. Believe me. I'm aware of the cancer community wherever I go. I could feel it at the Tour. People would come up to me before races or after races. I could feel it during the races. It's a community of shared experience. If you've ever belonged, you never leave."

Lance also knew that having cancer had changed his life in many ways, not the least of which was his ability to win stage races.

"If I never had cancer, I never would have won the Tour de France," he said, many times during his interviews. "I'm convinced of that. I wouldn't want to do it all over again, but I wouldn't change a thing, either. I'm talking to you today, but I'm not sure how. I know some things about cancer now. I know you have to pay attention, to watch for signs on your body, then react. I know you have to do research, go on the Internet, look for the second opinion, then the third, find out all your options. I also know you have to be lucky. That's probably as important as anything. I was very lucky."

Lance wasn't about to make a long and tiring trip home just to talk about winning a race. He felt he had a more important message to get across to the American public, while hopefully sparking more interest in cycling at the same time. In a strange way, the two distinctly different topics would always intersect with one another. He would continue to say that being a cancer survivor was the most important thing in his life, and he would continue to be the world's best stage racer. His good friend Jim Ochowicz confirmed what Lance had said—that in an unexpected way, having cancer and conquering it had also made him a better racer.

"The doubt about him had always been the climbs in the mountains," Ochowicz explained. "He always could sprint well, and he always was capable of winning a stage in the Tour. The mountains were his downfall. But with his weight loss—if you lose five pounds, that's a large weight loss for the mountains. It was all he needed. He became very good in the mountains."

Back in Europe, Lance continued to celebrate his victory in the traditional European way. He was feted wherever he went, and when he finally returned to the States for a much-deserved rest, he knew he had just begun his second career as a racer. Winning the Tour de France was the obvious pinnacle, but it didn't mean there were no more worlds to conquer. The Tour was a new world in itself each year, and almost as soon as he won the race, Lance knew he had to win it again. For one thing, he wanted to show that his 1999 victory wasn't a fluke. He also decided to make it a kind of anniversary. Each time he won the Tour it would mark another year as a cancer survivor.

For Lance, there was certainly newfound celebrity, endorsements, sponsors, people who wanted him for one thing or another. While Americans still didn't have an all-consuming interest in cycling, they seemed to have a special interest in Lance Armstrong. His story of survival, triumph in Paris, good looks, and commanding personality gave him a star quality reserved for a special few. Some felt he would get caught up in so many activities and demands for his time that his cycling would take a back seat. Those people didn't know the real Lance. From the moment he crossed the finish line at the Tour and raised his arms in triumph, he knew his goal would be to come back again. There were some important things, however, that his newfound status would allow him to do. If those things involved helping other cancer victims, then he would always take the time.

In early January of 2000, he wanted to set the record straight about something else. The whispers about the possibility of his using performance-enhancing drugs had never completely stopped. Though he knew there would always be skeptics, he still wanted to have his say. Nike and Lance got together to produce a documentary-style commercial called *Body*, which explored what was called his "steely resolve." There was footage of Lance riding, undergoing blood tests for drugs, and performing cardiovascular tests, as well as participating in a wind tunnel experiment to measure his cycling efficiency. His own voice-over allowed him to comment on everything taking place. During the footage, he said, in part, "This is my body and I can do whatever I want to it. I can push it, study it, tweak it, listen to it. Everybody wants to know what I'm on. What am I on? I'm on my bike, busting my ass six hours a day. What are you on?"

James Selmon, the director of *Body*, said he really got a sense of what Lance was like while putting together the footage. The essence of the shoot was to recreate Lance's drug-free ethic of hard work. "Yes, he's physically gifted as far as his lung capacity and all that," Selmon said, "but it's that extra hundred-and-ten percent that puts him over the top, as far as his ability to win [is concerned]."

In February of 2000, Lance launched the Cycle of Hope™, a national cancer-education campaign for both those with cancer and those at risk for developing the disease. To create the campaign, Lance teamed up with his non-profit foundation and the Bristol-Myers Squibb Company, the maker of the drugs that successfully treated his disease.

In effect, the Cycle of Hope was designed to support early cancer detection, reduce the fear associated with the disease, encourage a team approach to treatment, and foster hope in patients and their families. To help spread the word, Lance was featured in a national public service announcement that encouraged people to call a toll-free number or visit the campaign's Web site for the Cycle of Hope information packet. There was little doubt that Lance was committed to giving back to the community by helping other people cope with fighting the disease. His work in this area was extremely important to him.

"I ignored my symptoms until it was almost too late," he said. "I am dedicated to the Cycle of Hope campaign because I want to help others break out of their cycle of misunderstanding and fear, and empower themselves through the Cycle of Hope."

Even when he was giving time to his public service work and his foundation, Lance didn't stay off the bike for long. A world-class rider has to stay in training, keep his condition, then be ready to peak for the most important races. For Lance, that now meant the Tour de France. Yet despite his incredible victory in 1999, there were still naysayers. He wasn't even being spoken of as one of the favorites for the 2000 Tour. Many were focusing on two riders who had missed the race in '99: Germany's Jan Ullrich and Italy's Marco Pantini. Since they hadn't been in the race, people felt Lance still had to prove he could beat them. Other favorites were France's Richard Virenque and veterans Abraham Olano and Alexander Zulle, who had chased Lance for most of the race last year.

Lance knew it wouldn't be easy. Now everyone would be gunning for him. He would once again need his teammates on the U.S. Postal Service team. The team went to Europe in the spring to begin training in earnest and Lance entered some early-season events. He had mixed results, though he finished second at the Paris-Camembert race in April. Throughout April and May, he and his teammates trained in the mountains of France. Then, on May 5, his bid to become a two-time winner of the Tour almost came to a premature end.

He was training in the Pyrenees mountains, riding on the Hautacam, which would be one of the more difficult mountains climbs in the 2000 Tour. On the descent, Lance was traveling at high speed when his front tire hit a rock and popped. The bike hit a brick wall and Lance was thrown off the bike and into the wall. He hit headfirst. Even worse, he wasn't wearing his helmet. He had taken it off on the climb and forgotten to put it back for the descent. It was a frightening moment. Lance heard a ringing in his ears and felt the right side of his face beginning to swell up. One of his teammates called for an ambulance.

The worst of his injuries was just a slight concussion, but Lance was advised to take a couple of weeks off. To an athlete preparing for a major event, this can seem like an eternity. It could, however, have been worse, and Lance would never again forget to wear his helmet in practice. A month later, he was back on the Hautacam, completing the training schedule that had been interrupted by the crash. Once again, all his focus pointed to the Tour de France. In July, it was time to strut his stuff once more.

As usual, there was a highly competitive field, and a ton of reporters and media people were present. Most of them were asking the same questions: Could Lance Armstrong do it again? The course of the Tour is never the same two years in a row. In 2000, the course was mapped out to go counterclockwise around France, and it included some very difficult stages. It would open, as usual, with a time trial of just over ten miles. The riders wouldn't go into the mountains until stage ten. Lance and his teammates felt they were ready.

The Tour began with the time trial on July 1. Lance wanted to get off fast just as he had last year, and that meant winning the opening time trial. But when David Millar of Scotland sailed over the course with a blistering time of 19:03, Lance knew it wouldn't be easy. He attacked as always, and his time in the early going was better than the other competitors'. But by the halfway point, he was three seconds behind Millar. Once again, Lance picked up the pace and went as hard as he could to the finish line. When he looked at the clock, Millar had beaten him by two seconds. This time, Lance wouldn't be wearing the yellow jersey on the first day. But that didn't really matter. It was more important who would be wearing it on the *last* day.

This was a different race from last year's. For Lance, it was more tactical. He watched the riders whom he felt were the most dangerous and tried to stay ahead of them. He didn't win any of the first nine stages, and just before the Tour entered the mountains, he was in sixteenth place, almost six minutes behind the leader, Alberto Elli of Italy. At first glance, that didn't seem very good. But a closer look showed that Lance had set himself up in a very solid position. For openers, he was in front of the other top riders. He was forty-three seconds ahead of Ullrich and led Zulle by 4:05, Pantini by 5:12, and Virenque by 5:32. The tenth stage was a climb to Hautacam, where Lance had been injured the past May. It was a cold, rainy day, but Lance planned to launch an all-out attack. He knew most of the other riders didn't like the rain.

Lance felt as if it was going to be his day from the start. He had someone pulling him, as well. A Basque rider named Javier Otxoa, who was not in contention for the overall title, seemed to make this stage his personal Tour. He began attacking right from the start and opened up a huge lead. By the time Lance got ready for the final, steep climb to the Hautacam, Otxoa had a lead of 10:30, which seemed totally insurmountable. Lance was also on his own now. His teammates were all exhausted by the combination of the bad weather and the strenuous climb. Now Lance was riding in a chase group that included Pantini, Zulle, and Ullrich, as well as a number of other riders. All of them were way behind Otxoa, but Lance decided this was his time. He would not only try to destroy the rest of the field, but would also try to catch Otxoa.

Pantini and Zulle attacked first, but Lance took the cue and also attacked, passing both of them quickly. He then surged past another seven riders. Finally, only Otxoa remained in front of him. He surged again, then again, then once more. The gap of 10:30 had closed to 4:48 with five kilometers left. His coaches kept telling him the time through the two-way radio. With three kilometers left, Lance was within 3:21 of Otxoa. Another kilometer and he had cut the gap to 2:14. Though he continued to close the gap, there just wasn't enough course left. Otxoa crossed the finish line just forty-one seconds ahead of Lance. Lance hadn't won the stage, but when he looked at the times, he realized that he had just done something special.

Starting the day some six minutes behind the leader, he had not only made up every second of that, but had emerged from the climb with the yellow jersey once again his. He was now in the overall lead once again. In fact he already had opened a gap of 4:14 over Ullrich, considered the biggest threat to Lance's repeating his victory of a year earlier. With more mountain stages looming ahead of the riders, Lance Armstrong had once again become the favorite to win. His surge over the final miles had impressed some of the other veteran riders. Frenchman Raymond Poulidor, known as a strong climber himself, said Lance's final ascent was "unprecedented in the annals of cycling." Another French rider, Stephane Heulot, put it this way: "When I saw Armstrong I had the impression I was watching someone descending a hill I was trying to scale."

On another tortuous climb Lance found himself racing to the summit with Marco Pantini. They had broken away from the rest of the pack. Though he had the overall lead, Lance had not won a single stage. This one appeared to be well within his grasp. The two riders struggled through sharp wind and fatigue, with the finish line looming ahead. Lance, ahead of everyone but Pantini, suddenly slowed and allowed the Italian to win the stage. Once again, he was thinking about the politics of the Tour. It wasn't always the best idea to try to win too many stages, especially for the rider with the overall lead. He can be perceived as being greedy, as a slap in the face of the other riders.

It was something that Lance conceded Americans wouldn't understand. The mentality in the United States is to win, win, win. But when Pantini didn't take Lance's gesture in the spirit that it was offered, pronouncing after the race that Lance was simply not the strongest rider that day, Lance became angry. Next time, he'd be more choosy when he decided to concede a stage. Though Pantini would win another mountain stage a few days later, he had pretty much burned himself out. In stage sixteen, he weakened and fell back, finishing some thirteen minutes behind the lead group. The next day he withdrew from the Tour, citing stomach pains.

Lance was also tiring. Pantini had set a blistering pace before dropping back, and the other riders all paid the price. Lance lost 1:37 to Ullrich, but still led the German by more than five minutes. It was a scare, because at the end of that race he felt he had nothing left to give. He called it one of his worse days ever in a stage race. Fortunately, his will kept him from losing any more time.

Though there weren't as many rampant accusations of drug use against Lance in this

Tour, drugs were still one of the prime topics during the race. The talk of drugs made Lance recall reading a 1995 poll of mostly Olympic-caliber American athletes. According to the poll, more than fifty percent said they would take a drug that would enable them to become a champion, even though they knew there was a good chance that drug would kill them within five years.

"I've seen those results [of the poll], and I find them hard to believe," Lance said. "If they are true, then those people are crazy. Look, I live for cycling right now, but one day it's going to end, and then there are going to be no more yellow jerseys, no more adoration—we don't want your autograph, we don't want your picture, we don't want you to write a book. One day I'm going to be a normal guy, and that's going to be fine."

It was just another way of Lance reiterating that he wouldn't take a performance-enhancing drug that could harm his body. His secret wasn't really a secret—it was just constant, intense training. He put in the work, the hours on the bike, something that his wife could attest to easily.

"For nine months out of the year it's like we're living in a monastery," Kristen Armstrong said, describing how Lance spent up to seven hours on his bike some days. "[Then] he comes home just like any other guy comes home. The first thing he always says is, 'Where's my boy!' He doesn't look tired. He looks so happy and peaceful. Then he has a bite, naps, has dinner, spends a few hours around the house and goes to bed. And that's that. Day in, day out, that's how we live. People see the highlights, but they don't see that it's a very, very serious commitment."

In effect, Lance was simply outworking everyone else; no frills, no secret methods, and no drugs. And now, another victory was well within his grasp. Despite his lead, however, he was concerned after stage sixteen because he had felt so exhausted. He felt that Ullrich was still a threat, especially if he showed any weakness. If the other riders perceived that he was weakening, there would be a feeding frenzy to catch him. He also wanted to win at least one stage. It just didn't seem right to win the overall Tour without winning a stage. That opportunity finally came in the nineteenth stage and final time trial. It would be 58.5 kilometers at full speed.

On this day, Lance had it. He felt good as soon as he began, and he attacked the course. He didn't stop until he crossed the finish line, winning the stage by twenty-five seconds and roaring over the course with an average speed of

53.98 kilometers per hour. It was the second fastest time trial speed ever, just behind the record set by the other American winner, Greg LeMond. Lance felt it was imperative to make the statement he had just made.

"It's important for the [rider wearing the yellow jersey] to show himself in the time trial because it's the race of truth," Lance said. "So it would have been easy to ride easy and ride conservative and not take risks, but I think it's important for the race leader to make that demonstration. I really wanted to win this stage. I had a lot of stress and a lot of anger and a lot of pressure. The Tour wouldn't be complete for me if I won the Tour without winning a stage."

When Lance held on to his solid lead during the next stage, he had once again all but won the race. Now came the ceremonial final ride to Paris and his second straight Tour de France victory, the one that should have silenced the skeptics once and for all.

10

Going for a Triple

Every Tour de France victory is special in its own right. Lance once again had all kinds of feelings as he crossed the finish line to repeat his victory of a year earlier. He proved once again that he had indeed become the best, a thought echoed by the second-place finisher, Jan Ullrich.

"Armstrong is a worthy champion," Ullrich said. "He was the strongest man, and he met our every attack. He earned his victory."

The detractors were slowly melting away, but for the moment Lance didn't care about that. He sought out his family, hugged them, then lofted his nine-month-old son, Luke, above his head. He had tears in his eyes.

"This one's even more special than last year,

partly because of this little guy," he said.

It was a victory with a contradiction of a sort. In one sense, Lance said it was more difficult than the year before since the course was more physically demanding, with four very difficult mountain stages through the Alps and Pyrenees. He said he was a more tired athlete this time. Mentally, however, he admitted it wasn't as difficult as the first time around.

"I was mentally exhausted at the end of last year's Tour," he said, "partly because of all the controversy and accusations. This year has been much more positive, a real vindication in many ways, and I can carry all that positive energy into the Olympics."

Lance's next goal was already the 2000 Summer Olympics in Sydney, Australia. He was pointing toward winning a gold medal in the time trial event.

"Winning gold is a big objective," he admitted in an interview just after the Tour ended. But he also told reporters that no matter how successful he was on his bike, he still had a purpose in life that would always override everything else.

"The fight against cancer is still my biggest ambition," he said. "It's nice to win the Tour de France, and to win it a second time, but [helping to fight cancer] is something that will be going on when I'm fifty."

Lance didn't need any special encouragement to continue his campaign to help with cancer research and encourage cancer patients. He continued to be an inspiration to many people. There weren't a whole lot of Americans on the Champs-Elysées to see Lance cross the finish line, but those who were there were not only rooting for him, but full of admiration for what he had accomplished and what he stood for. One spectator, Kevin Fink from Denton, Maryland, expressed his thoughts to an American reporter. "Everybody knows somebody who's suffering from, or died from, cancer—and everybody knows he beat a terrible case of cancer," the man said. "It's frankly just amazing to see him participating, never mind dominating the sport. He gives everyone a feeling of hope."

Lance returned home for another round of interviews and to make some appearances for his sponsors. He and Kristen went to New York, Los Angeles, then Austin. They then returned to Nice, France, so that Lance could begin training for the Olympics. Coming so soon after the Tour made it difficult. He had to regain his fitness and then peak in time for Sydney. What he didn't count on was the bane of all cyclists at one time or another—a car in the wrong place at the wrong time.

About a month before the Olympics, Lance

was training on a narrow, twisting road where he rarely saw any cars. He knew the mountain roads well, and in all the years he had trained there, said he had never seen any cars on the particular stretch where he was riding. He was moving at a very fast pace and taking a sharp turn when suddenly there was a car coming right at him. There was absolutely no time to react. It was a head-on and Lance went into the air.

Lance literally flew over the hood of the car and landed in the road, headfirst. This time, Lance was wearing a helmet and felt he had come through the accident without real injury. His bike had been mangled, but he felt no bones were broken and the helmet had protected his head. Lance called Kristen on his cell phone and asked her to come pick up his fellow rider and him. He told his wife he was all right, but when he awoke the next morning, he wasn't.

The pain in his neck and upper shoulders was severe. Lance couldn't turn his head and felt sharp, stabbing pains every time he moved. Kristen drove him to the hospital where an MRI revealed a fracture of the C-7 vertebra. In layman's terms, Lance had a broken neck. Suddenly, the best cyclist in the world was a questionable choice for the Olympics. But in Lance's mind, he was riding in Sydney, no matter what. When he got back on the bike, he found he still couldn't turn his head easily, which made it difficult for him to see things on both sides. But he could ride straight ahead, train, and improve his fitness as his neck slowly improved. When he made the trip to Sydney about a week before the start of the Olympics, he admitted he was probably about eighty percent healthy.

The two Olympic cycling events were a daylong road race and a time trial. The road race was on a flat course that favored sprinters, and Lance didn't feel his chances for a medal were that good. But he hoped he could attack quickly in the time trial and then gut it out to take the gold. That's where he was pinning his Olympic hopes. When he could do no better than thirteenth in the road race, an event won by Jan Ullrich, he focused even more on winning the time trial.

By the time it was his turn in the time trial, one of his U.S. Postal teammates, Vyacheslav Ekimov, was in first place with a very fast time of fifty-seven minutes and forty seconds. Lance started out quickly and with his usual focus and determination. But as he sprinted through the course he knew he was losing time to Ekimov, falling behind. He was going as fast as he possibly could that day, and it just wasn't good enough. When he crossed the finish line he was thirty-three seconds behind Ekimov's time and twenty-six seconds behind Ullrich, who finished second. Lance managed third for a bronze medal, but it was disappointing, nevertheless.

"I came to win the gold medal," Lance admitted, "but I did everything I could. I went as hard as I could. My heart rate was pegged the whole time. I could not have gone any harder. I'm glad the race is over and I can enjoy myself. I had hoped to make it a double celebration but I can't complain."

The other celebration was the October 2 anniversary of Lance's cancer diagnosis. It had now been four years. "Every year we have a party or have some special time with friends and family," Lance said. "They've occurred all over the world, sometimes in Austin, sometimes in France, and this year in Sydney."

No one can win them all, not even Lance Armstrong. Had he not had the neck injury a month before the Olympics, he might have fared better. But then again, maybe he just wouldn't have been good enough that day. In truth, Lance's focus had changed. He had really geared all his racing efforts toward winning one race, the Tour de France. If he won others, that was fine. He certainly had the ability on any given day to win almost any cycling race, but his talents as he had honed them were made for the most grueling stage race of them all. The mountains had been his weakness in the early days of his career, before his illness. Now, he was without a doubt the very best mountain rider and climber in the world. His competitors in the Tour knew that even if he didn't seem to be near the lead, once the race reached the mountain stages everyone else had better look over their shoulders. Lance Armstrong was coming.

It was no different in 2001. All his efforts again pointed to the Tour, where he would try to become the first American to win the race three consecutive times. He didn't waver from his intense training schedule and his goal to come into the Tour even stronger than he had been the two previous years. The U.S. Postal team added two new riders, both climbing specialists, with the objective to give Lance even more support when the big race arrived. Everyone was once again geared for Lance to again wear the yellow jersey as he rode down the Champs-Elysées.

As usual, he entered a number of early-season races for the purpose of conditioning, not necessarily to win. In April he rode in one of his favorite races, Amstel Gold, and ended up in a two-man sprint with Erik Dekker. The two rode together over the final miles of the race and, in the final burst to the finish line, Dekker was the winner. Lance simply said that his rival was the better man that day.

Then, just a couple of weeks before the Tour, Lance entered the Tour of Switzerland. He started it by winning the Prologue time trial and stayed among the leaders right up to the mountain time trial a week later. When he won that, he was in the overall lead and he held it the rest of the way. There was little doubt that he was ready to defend his title in the Tour de France.

With a number of the top cyclists recovering from injuries and a couple of others not in good form, only Jan Ullrich was considered a major threat to Lance. This time, he was the clear favorite. He served notice that he was ready when he finished second in the Tour's Prologue time trial. Then, as had become his pattern, he rode comfortably through the early stages, just setting back and seemingly waiting for the mountain stages to begin. At one point he was in twenty-fourth place, and after nine stages he was still only twenty-third. Those who didn't know him might have figured he didn't have it this year. After all, if there were twenty-some-odd riders ahead of him, a few of them might be able to hold him off. However, those familiar with the Tour and the riders, and with

Lance's ability, knew how quickly things could change once he got into the mountains. But no one was prepared for what he was about to do in the next two stages of the race.

The first mountain stage was the famed climb up to the Alpe d'Huez. The riders were on their bikes for some six hours when they came to the base of the final, twelve-mile climb, a brutally steep and daunting task for any rider. Lance was riding near the rear of the peloton, and to the other riders he appeared to be winded and out of breath. That was all part of the plan. All of a sudden he looked directly at Ullrich. Those seeing it said it was a cold stare, a challenge he knew couldn't be answered, not by Ullrich, not by anyone. With that, Lance began to climb, perhaps as he never had before.

When he began his attack, France's Laurent Roux was the stage leader, some six minutes ahead of Lance. Yet within an incredibly short amount of time he passed Roux, who later said, "I had the feeling I was being passed by a motorcycle." Lance continued to attack the steep grade and his opponents. Ullrich tried to go with him, but simply couldn't keep up. Finally, Lance crossed the finish line for his first stage win of the Tour. He had blown away the field, winning the race by two full minutes over the second-place finisher. In fact, he beat one rider by an incredible forty-two minutes. Seven riders never even finished the tortuous climb.

Lance still wasn't the overall leader, but he was getting much closer. He knew he had expended a huge amount of energy, maybe too much; he commented, "I may pay for this." He was concerned because the next stage was a mountain time trial, where the riders go individually up a mountain as fast as they possibly can. It was called "The Ride of Truth," to the top of Chamrousse, the ski resort where the legendary Jean-Claude Killy won three gold medals in the 1968 Olympics. Only this time the headlines were made by Lance Armstrong.

Once again he attacked the course, his legs pumping, his body not wavering, his form almost perfect. When he reached the top he had the best time of the day, giving him another stage win and bringing him even closer to the overall lead. The frightening part for the other riders was that his main rivals for the overall title were already behind him. Those in front of him must have known that a riding machine was getting ready to blow them away. Perhaps it was one of his teammates, Tyler Hamilton, who put it best after Lance's two straight stage wins.

"American doesn't understand," Hamilton said. "What [Lance] did here these last two days was like John Elway winning those two Super Bowls."

When Lance returned to Kristen after winning the two stages, she showed him a letter from her obstetrician. She had once again undergone in-vitro fertilization with the sperm Lance had preserved before his chemo treatments. Both of them anxiously opened the letter and couldn't believe the news. Test results confirmed that the in-vitro fertilization had worked again. Not only that, this time Kristen was carrying twin girls! The two of them were overjoyed, and Lance had further motivation to go on and win his third Tour.

When the thirteenth stage of the race had arrived, Lance was in third place overall. He was four minutes ahead of Ullrich, but still nine minutes behind François Simon, the race leader. This was another hard climb to a jagged summit called Col du Portet d'Aspet, followed by a steep, dangerous descent. It was the same route where Lance's former teammate with Motorola, Fabio Casartelli, had been killed six years earlier. As expected, Lance left everyone behind on the climb. As he sped down the descent and past the memorial that marked the spot where Fabio had been killed, he said he felt a surge of confidence.

"I knew I was going to win that day," he said, later.

He not only won, but he made up so much time that he once again emerged as the overall leader. It was his third stage win over the last four stages and, for the first time in the 2001 Tour, he was wearing the yellow jersey. There probably wasn't another rider in the field who didn't think the jersey would stay where it now sat for the remainder of the Tour, on the back of Lance Armstrong.

In the fourteenth stage, yet another climb, this time to Luz-Ardiden, Ullrich made a last-ditch effort to attack. His respect for Lance had grown since during stage thirteen. He had taken a fall and, seeing that, Lance slowed his charge, waiting for Ullrich to get back up on the bike before continuing. It was a great gesture of sportsmanship. This time when Ullrich attacked, Lance pulled up even with him and the two rode together to the finish line. Neither would win the stage, but as they crossed the line together, Ullrich extended his right hand and Lance took it. Ullrich would later say his gesture was a concession, as well as one of respect. He knew now that he simply couldn't win, that no one could beat Lance Armstrong.

The rest of the race was almost a formality. Lance won the eighteenth stage and an individual time trial, then two days later once again rode down the Champs-Elysées at the head of his U.S. Postal team and crossed the line as the winner for a third straight time. He finished some six minutes and forty-four seconds ahead of Ullrich, a sizeable margin of victory. He had also completed the entire course in eighty-six hours, seventeen minutes, and twenty-eight seconds, making his the third-fastest Tour in the history of the race. There was little doubt now about his place in history. No matter what happened in the future, his name would always be synonymous with the Tour de France. He was now one of only eight riders to have won the Tour three times, and one of just five who had won three in a row.

There is an expression for a dominant Tour rider, one that is reserved for a special few. They are called the *patron,* the unquestioned boss of the peloton. The patron can be described as "a dominant personality who commands favors, respect, even fear from the other riders in the Tour. He admonishes and badgers, bestows blessings and bears grudges."

It was said that there hadn't been a true patron since the great Bernard Hinault's last Tour in 1986. Was Lance now falling into that role? He didn't seem to think so, perhaps more because of changing times. "I think the days of the true patrons are over," he said. "There are a lot of leaders, a lot of guys who command a lot of respect. Maybe I'm one of those."

Lance certainly had the respect of former champions. Eddy Merckx, who won the Tour five times and had known Lance for some time, marveled at his skills and tenacity. "Armstrong could win five, he could win six, he could win seven," Merckx said, "as long as he stays focused on the Tour de France."

Johan Bruyneel, director of the U.S. Postal Service team, felt that Lance's achievements and abilities could no longer be ignored by the other riders. "It's been a long time since cycling had a real boss," Bruyneel said. "Right now in the Tour de France, people consider Lance the boss."

Italian rider Davide Bramati echoed those thoughts when he said, "[Lance] is the big sheriff. He is the law in the peloton."

But there was still some backlash, perhaps because of the culture clash of an American dominating a traditional European event with old European values. The Tour's general director, Jean-Marie Leblanc, criticized Lance in a French newspaper, citing, among other things, his lack of "warmth, " his unwillingness to speak French, and his decision to employ a pair of bodyguards that Leblanc referred to as "gorillas."

Lance replied by saying, "I've really tried to respect the event and the French people."

While staying in Nice he often signed autographs and did interviews in French, though he admitted, "the little French I do have is brutal and ugly and sparse."

The French fans, who represent the majority of spectators watching the Tour, also seemed to harbor some resentments against Lance, though some of that can come under the category of sour grapes. A number of French riders were found to be using illegal drugs while Lance, the American who was dominating their most prized sporting event, had always tested clean and continued to do so. There were still many people who simply could not believe that he could be so dominant without using something to enhance his performance.

Most of them just didn't know of the intensity with which Lance trained, the enormous amount of work he put in every year while preparing for the Tour. Johan Bruyneel recalled a training session the previous May, when Lance rode hard up the Col de Madeleine, a mountain course, on a rainy day. At the top, Bruyneel opened his car door, ready to load the bike on top and give Lance a ride back home. He already had a hot cup of tea ready to give him.

"Anyone else would have gotten in the car, had some hot tea and gone home," Bruyneel said. "Lance just turned his bike around, rode to the bottom of the Madeleine and went up it again, just so he could get another big climb that day."

In some ways, Lance will probably always remain a "foreign" presence within the Tour. But even if some fans couldn't appreciate the full depth of his talents, the other riders could. Dutch rider Erik Dekker, a world-class rider who won three stages during the 2000 Tour, said this about the man he could never catch: "I am very passionate about cycling, but I cannot match Lance. Mentally, he is unique."

11

Can Lance Tie the Record?

Three in a row! For an American cyclist, winning the Tour de France three straight times seemed tantamount to the impossible. But Lance Armstrong had triumphed. Moreover, he appeared to have evolved into the perfect Tour de France rider. All his energies pointed to this one race and his preparation was meticulous. Even the legendary Eddy Merckx had said there was no limit to how many Lance might win if he stayed focused on the Tour. It hadn't taken him long after winning number three to announce he'd go after a fourth in 2002. But how many races after that? Could he go even further, continuing to fend off the best cyclists in the world?

"I may get to the end of [next year's] Tour de France and say, 'Man, I've just had enough; I'm outta here,'" Lance said. "Ultimately, I want to decide when I leave [the sport]. It's not going to be because of a win or a loss. It will just be between me and my family. Then I'll say, 'You know what? It's been great. See ya later.'"

It certainly wasn't time yet. Soon it was back to training with Lance's singular focus already pointing toward the nest year's Tour de France. Unfortunately, he was still hounded by accusations claiming that he used performance-enhancing drugs, even though he was tested often and had never once come up positive. In fact, French authorities were supposedly still investigating reports from two years earlier that claimed U.S. Postal team members had been seen disposing of what appeared to be medical waste from the team's hotel. The investigation, like others, would go nowhere, and Lance said that it was a shame that France and its many cycling fans would have to endure another Tour with a cloud hanging over it.

He released a statement once again calling the Tour de France "the greatest athletic event in the world." Yet the periodic suspicions and allegations made it seem as if some people still couldn't believe that a cancer survivor, a man who had a terribly advanced case of the disease, could come back and win the Tour three straight times without some kind of outside help. And when he appeared at the starting line in July of 2002 to try for a fourth straight victory, he still heard occasional cries of *"Dop-AY! Dop-AY!"* ("Doped! Doped!") from some unfriendly fans. It was probably something he would always have to endure despite there not being the slightest hint of proof that he had ever taken anything illegal.

When he began the defense of his title by winning the Prologue time trial, many of his opponents seemed instantly deflated. It was almost a case of "here we go again!" As was his custom, Lance didn't press hard in the early stages, just keeping a close eye on his toughest rivals while letting those who really didn't have a chance at the overall title take the stage victories. But when he finished second in the ninth stage, the extended time trial—and still wasn't wearing the leader's yellow jersey—it seemed to embolden some of his competitors. In fact, Spain's Igor Gonzalez de Galdeano, who was leading the race at the time and wearing the yellow jersey, brashly announced, "The Tour has changed."

The statement, obviously, was referring to the fact that other cyclists were catching up to

Lance. Two days later, the riders entered Stage Eleven, a climb from Genoble to Chamrousse. Gonzalez de Galdeano still wore the yellow jersey, but had just a twenty-six-second lead on Lance. As was his style, Lance attacked the climb, showing great heart, talent, drive, and of course his unshakable will. He blew away the other riders and emerged not only as the stage winner, but wearing the yellow jersey as well. And when he won a second straight mountain stage the next day, he increased his lead even more.

The Tour has changed! The only way it changed was that Lance Armstrong had become more dominant than ever. Back home, people like hockey legend Wayne Gretzky were singing his praises. Gretzky, known as "The Great One" for his hockey prowess, compared Lance to basketball's Michael Jordan and golf's Tiger Woods, adding, "There's not a question that Lance Armstrong belongs with those two guys. Not only because of what he has done as an athlete, but also what he has been able to come back from."

As for Lance, he simply wanted to win, and when a reporter asked if perhaps his dominance was not good for the Tour, he replied quickly, "I know that I love the race. I love everything it stands for. It is what they pay me to do. This is my job. [Winning the Tour] is what the team wants, what the sponsors want, what cycling fans in America want, what cancer survivors around the world want."

Finally, Lance took the individual time trial during Stage Nineteen, his fourth stage win of the Tour, all but insuring his fourth straight victory. The ceremonial ride the down Champs-Elysées made it official. He had done it again, beating back his challengers, one by one, both physically and mentally, until there was no one left.

This time he had won by more than seven minutes over his closest rival, and in doing so had achieved cycling immortality. Not only would his name forever be mentioned alongside the greats of the sport—Merckx, Hinault, Indurain—but he was almost making it look easy. After it was over, he spoke again about how much this difficult event meant to him.

"It's an honor and it makes me happy to be able to win again," Lance said. "It's what I devote my life to. If I lost this race, I would be extremely disappointed. Much more disappointed than anyone can guess. It was a long three weeks. With so many mountains, it was hard on the head as well as the legs. It's hard to know the significance of it. I just live for the moment."

Even many of the French fans, who wanted to dislike this American for taking over their race, had come to admire his talent.

"A man's value is in his spirit, not his country, and Armstrong is a super champion," said Dominique Audusseau, a wine dealer who was a huge cycling fan. "I adore the guy. He'll be the first to win six Tours."

There were others, though, who still felt that Lance was somewhat aloof, unlike the European cyclists and even some Americans. He would often go back to his trailer after a stage was over instead of mingling with the fans and often isolated himself behind his bodyguards, as if he didn't want any part of the crowds. But in truth, Lance was first and foremost an athlete, with a single-minded concentration on the task at hand. He had a routine that he followed carefully throughout the grueling race, and he didn't want it interrupted by anything or anyone. As Lance said, answering his critics, "This is not theater; it's sport. I believe in performance and the beauty of the race."

The Tour de France had, in effect, become the Tour de Lance. The question was once again, how long could he go on? Since only Miguel Indurain had won five straight Tours, there was little doubt that Lance would return in 2003 and try to match the mark set by the great Spanish racer. But before Lance began training for 2003 he had a shocking announcement, something no one saw coming. In February, Lance and Kristin declared publicly that they were separating. They would eventually have a brief reconciliation in June, but by September decide to file for divorce. Because of Lance's high profile and all the publicity that had surrounded their marriage and subsequent births of their children, both felt they had to be open about what had happened.

Kristen released a statement saying that their marital problems were "brought on gradually by a number of pressures, rather than one big blow-up. We've been together four and a half years, and we've had six homes, three languages, three countries, one cancer comeback, three children, four Tour de France wins, and one rise to celebrity. You're not supposed to cram such a huge amount of events into such a small period of time."

Their lives certainly weren't what are usually considered "normal." Besides his celebrity standing, Lance had to spend an inordinate amount of time training, and training hard. The pressures to also have a family life had to be enormous. Both Lance and Kristin agreed the most important thing was to maintain a healthy environment for their children.

Splitting up may have been difficult, but working together for the good of the children wasn't. In fact, after their divorce in September, Lance would say, "The craziest thing is, we're closer now and better friends than ever before. We're fully committed to maintaining a good relationship, but not a marriage."

Both had to move on and make the best of it. It couldn't have been easy for either of them. In Lance's case, the separation and attempted reconciliation came at a time when he was training hard to try to win a record-tying fifth consecutive Tour. To a sports-loving public, both in the United States and Europe, that's all they really cared about. Could Lance do it? There were questions everywhere. Chris Carmichael, Lance's coach, was asked about how the body reacts during the Tour, and he wrote an interesting story about the Tour de France diet.

In it, he explained that riders consume an average of six to seven thousand calories a day, more on the days that are particularly long and hard. Some are taken in during regular sit-down meals. There is breakfast, which is the pre-race meal, and then dinner. The remainder is consumed while on the bike during the race and through some snacking between meals. As Carmichael remarked, "No matter the time of day, it is rare to see a Tour de France rider without either food or drink in his hand."

Not surprisingly, 70 percent of the calories Lance consumed were from carbohydrates, with just 15 percent from protein and the other 15 percent from fats. Carbohydrates serve as the primary fuel for any aerobic sport. As the intensity of that performance increases, the percentage of calories needed from carbs increases as well. They are the only fuel both the brain and central nervous system can use, and if the percentage isn't just right, the rider can "bonk," causing confusion, nausea, and disorientation. So it's a delicate balancing act, even more so than with marathon runners (who traditionally "carb load" before a race) or even triathletes. Those two events are over in a day. The Tour lasts three weeks, and every day the miles pile up, leading to exhaustion.

The carbs come from potatoes, rice, pasta, cereals, whole grain breads, and fruits and vegetables. Proteins include eggs, meat, chicken, and yogurt, while the fat intake is controlled by the way the meals are prepared. Sports drinks, as well as water, are also important. The specially formulated sports drinks not only provides more carbs, but are also a source of all important electrolytes, which are lost when the body perspires. If an electrolyte balance is not maintained, the rider can cramp. So competing in the Tour—let alone winning it—is a lot more than being able to pedal fast. Every detail counts, and diet is important.

There were several other factors leading up to the 2003 Tour that had to be considered. Lance was just a few months from turning thirty-two years old. For a stage-race cyclist, this could be a cause for concern. Riders with youth on their side often have an advantage. Because he was derailed by his illness, Lance had gotten a late start, and some wondered if age could affect him, slow him down just enough to make him vulnerable. His personal situation with Kristen couldn't have made it any easier. Normally, extra personal burdens do not enable a rider to compete with maximum efficiency. But then again, Lance Armstrong is no ordinary athlete.

In the 2003 race, it was widely acknowledged that Lance's biggest competition would come from Germany's Jan Ullrich, who had won the Tour in 1997 and was also a four-time runner-up. He was coming off a disastrous 2002 season in which he was not only cited for drunk driving, but had tested positive for an illegal party drug, served a racing ban, then underwent two knee surgeries. He wanted nothing more than to win a second Tour and dethrone Lance Armstrong in the process. It was a friendly but fierce competition.

Right from the start Lance knew that in the 2003 Tour, a triumphant ride down the Champs-Elysées was not going to be easy. First, he came down with a stomach flu just days before the start of the race. There was an even stronger hint of what was to come when he finished an uncharacteristic seventh in the Prologue time trail. Though he was just seven seconds behind the winner, he didn't like it. Then came Stage One. Lance was riding in a crowded pack when everyone began sprinting toward the finish line. There was a terrible crash, a tangle of bikes and riders. It was Lance's first crash since 1999. His bike was wrecked, but he came away with just a tweaked back. Teammate Levi Leipheimer had to drop out of the race with injuries while another teammate, Tyler Hamilton, suffered a broken collarbone. In the spirit of the Tour, Hamilton would continue riding and complete the entire race.

In the first mountain stages—Seven, Eight, and Nine—Lance rode well enough to take over the yellow jersey, but unlike past years he hadn't delivered the knockout punch yet. Ullrich was hanging with him, as were several other riders. There was another close call in Stage Nine as the riders came out of the Alps.

Spanish rider Joseba Beloki took a corner too fast and lost control of his bike. The crash sent Beloki out of the competition with a broken leg, and Lance had to turn into a hay field to avoid hitting Beloki's bike. He needed all his handling skills to keep from crashing, even vaulting over a deep ditch before rejoining the race. This wasn't the way it was supposed to go.

And the problems weren't over yet. Stage Twelve was another time trial in which Lance almost always excelled. This time, however, he weakened midway through. He was dehydrating under a scorching sun and wilted at the end, finishing second. He had lost nearly eleven pounds during the race. He had also lost ninety-six precious seconds to Ullrich, who not only won the stage, but beat Lance in the time trial for the first time ever. Some saw this as the beginning of the end, that Lance's age might be catching up with him. But whenever things looked bleak and people began writing him off, they tended to forget Lance's uncompromising will to win.

Now it was all on the line. After the time trial, the riders would head into the Pyrenees Mountains for the next four stages. While Lance still wore the leader's yellow jersey, he had both Ullrich and Alexandre Vinokourov breathing down his neck. Then in the first two stages of the Pyrenees, his rivals attacked repeatedly and Lance barely held onto the lead. It was very tight; only fifteen seconds separated Lance from Ullrich, with Vinokourov three seconds behind that. It was one of the closest competitions in years, and Lance had not shown signs of breaking it open.

Then came the all-important Stage Fifteen. Had Lance faltered and his rivals moved past him, who knows what could have happened. Lance attacked with renewed vigor as Ullrich struggled to keep up. As the two riders battled on a mist-covered 8.3-mile climb to the Pyrenean ski station of Luz-Ardiden, riding on a narrow road with fans on both sides, Lance's handlebar caught a spectator's bag, causing him to fall. He landed on his back, but the bike was okay. Being the sportsman he was, Ullrich stopped riding until Lance could get back on the bike. The two then resumed their battle, with Lance pulling away down the stretch to win the stage in dramatic fashion. Vinokourov finished farther back and was all but eliminated. Now Lance led Ullrich by just one minute and seven seconds, which was surely better than fifteen seconds.

It finally all came down to Stage Nineteen, the final time trial, when the cyclists ride alone against the clock. The day was rainy, the roads slick and slippery. Lance wouldn't win the stage, but Ullrich's time suffered too when his bike skidded on the wet road and crashed with just a short distance to go. On the final day, Lance was able to cruise in for the win. He had tied Indurain's record of five straight Tours, but had done it by just a scant sixty-one seconds more than Ullrich. Never before had he won the race by less than six minutes. But to prove how tough the competition was getting, Lance's average speed over the three-week race was 25.38 mph, the fastest in Tour history, breaking his own record.

While he was overjoyed at winning this difficult Tour, he admitted afterward that he wasn't at his best.

"This was absolutely the most difficult year for many reasons," he said. "Being this close makes it feel different, feel better than all the others. It's very satisfying. When I heard that Jan had crashed [I knew] the race was finished. I took it easy and really took no risks. But I said at the beginning that he was the biggest challenger. He gave us a lot of problems. Jan is back to his highest levels and nobody makes me more motivated than Jan Ullrich. He's a big champion."

Then Lance admitted that he felt early on that this would be a difficult Tour to win. "I knew before the Prologue in Paris that it was going to be close," he explained. "[But] I didn't expect it to come down to the last decisive stages. This is a bit of a surprise. I had a lot of luck. I'd always rather be lucky than good. But I don't plan on being this vulnerable next year. I won't make the same mistakes again."

So it seemed he was already announcing his intent to try for a record-breaking sixth straight Tour de France win. Ullrich also made it clear he would be returning in 2004 with a goal of dethroning the king. "I delivered one of the best races ever," the German star said. "This time I was very close to Armstrong. The next time . . . I will be even better prepared."

The former greats of the sport were also busy analyzing Lance's victory and putting his accomplishments into perspective. "Armstrong's courageous, a fighter, somebody who perseveres until the end," said five-time winner Bernard Hinault of France. "You have to do like him to beat him. He's certainly a star, but I don't know if he's a superstar. It's a new generation of riders. They have radios. They work more closely in teams. It's a different era."

It isn't unusual for athletes from one era to cite changes in a sport. That's why it is often difficult to make comparisons. Sports change. But Spain's Miguel Indurain, whose record

Lance had just tied, cited an old criticism when he said he felt Belgium's Eddy Merckx was still the greatest cyclist ever.

"Merckx competed in virtually every cycling competition," Indurain said, "whereas Armstrong really only focuses on the Tour." Indurain went on to say that he felt Lance would have a tough time winning a sixth straight Tour. "Of course, it's possible. But every year it gets more difficult, and he'll face some tough rivals." Though maybe it was wishful thinking on Indurian's part, because his record would indeed be broken.

As for Lance, he was already motivated to go again. He received a congratulatory phone call from President George W. Bush and once again said the close finish was already motivating him.

"The other years I won by six, seven minutes," he said. "I think it makes it more exciting and sets up an attempt for number six. This Tour took a lot out of me. So I need to step back from cycling and from the races, relax a little bit, then focus on 2004 in due time."

His fans couldn't wait.

12

Riding into History

No one really knew what had caused the close finish in the 2003 Tour. Some suggested Lance was not as well-prepared as he had been in the past, or that the competition was catching up with him. There was also the age factor, not to mention the changes in his personal life. Shortly after the Tour ended, Lance and Kristin decided to separate for good.

That October, Lance's personal life changed. Appearing at a Grand Slam for Children event in Las Vegas, he met the popular, Grammy-award-winning rock singer Sheryl Crow. The two hit it off, and by the end of the year, when Lance and Kristin were officially divorced, his new relationship became public. He and Kristin continued to work together to make sure they remained close to their children. At the same time Lance seemed happy in his new relationship.

He also continued to devote much of his time to his foundation and serving as an inspiration for cancer patients everywhere. By 2004 the organization had moved from a three-story house to a large office building in Austin. And from just a handful of employees at the start, there were now forty-five staff members and hundreds of volunteers, working for a common goal. Letters poured in for Lance every day from those who had survived cancer and from those looking for hope and inspiration. The foundation also helps raise money for cancer research and its work is ongoing and constant. In 2004, the foundation began to distribute the thin yellow bracelets with the words LIVE-STRONG inscribed on the band. It is a play on Lance's name and spirit, and the bracelets have become an integral part of the foundation's fund-raising activities.

Bianca Bellavia, communications director at the foundation since 1999, said that Lance was humbled by the letters from cancer patients. "I think it becomes a motivating factor for him," she said. "He's often said he thinks of all those people who are undergoing therapy and treatment for cancer when he's on those mountain stages."

The individual stories of cancer patients who have been inspired by Lance continue to be endless. There's also no doubt that his consecutive Tour de France wins had given him a high celebrity profile, providing a platform that enabled him to influence those who delegated money for cancer research. In that sense, it's a winning combination to have a guy who appreciated and made the most of a second chance at life and wasn't about to forget others going through the same ordeal. For that, Lance Armstrong deserves the admiration of everyone.

But back to the bike. Once again, Lance pointed toward his trademark race, and in 2004 wanted to be sure that he was fully prepared. While cycling still continued as a relatively minor sport in the United States, all eyes became focused when it was Tour de France time, and that was because of one man—Lance Armstrong.

More people than ever were talking about the Tour and the kind of event it was. Many of them spoke from experience.

"A champion has to have the physical gift from God," said Jonathan Boyer, who was the first American to ever ride the Tour. "But he also needs the mental stamina and drive and emotional stability to win the race. The Tour pushes your body further than it has ever gone."

In 1985, Boyer won the 3,120-mile Race Across America in nine days, two hours, and six seconds. He would sleep for just a couple of hours each night. Yet he said the Tour de France was a more intense event. The Race Across America, he said, "is long and difficult, but you don't go fast enough to build up real fatigue in your muscles."

Former racer Laurent Jalabert, who has done commentary for the Tour, might have summed it up best when he said, "Nobody who has not done it can understand the scale of the exploit."

Lance understood, maybe better than anybody. Though he prepared meticulously for every single stage, he said that essentially he would break the race down into three main sections. During the first third of the race, he explained, "You have nothing to gain, but everything to lose." You can fall victim to a crash, the weather, old-fashioned bad luck. The midsection of the race, encompassing most of the mountain stages, is where you "learn who has done their homework." That's when Lance always tried to break his opponents and take charge of the race. In the final part of the race, if you have built a cushion, you simply ride conservatively, stay away from trouble, but maintain your lead. For Lance, it was a formula that was obviously working.

Yet despite his enormous success, preparation, and obvious ability, he never approached the Tour de France feeling overconfident and predicting victory. "Every year I'm nervous before I begin," he said. "There are always doubts and fears because you know that no matter how well prepared you are, something unexpected can always happen."

Finally, it was time for the 2004 Tour and a chance at six consecutive wins. Lance roared out of the gate, finished a close second in the opening time trial, and was already leading his main rivals. He then seized the yellow jersey early and this time wasn't about to let go. Following his formula of dividing the race into three sections, he blew away his rivals in the mountains, winning three stage victories in the Alps, including a time trial on the now-legendary climb to L'Alpe d'Huez. Then he took yet another stage in the Pyrenees. By the time the riders came out of the mountains, the race was no longer in doubt. It wouldn't be the way it was in 2003— close right up until the end. Ullrich couldn't keep up this time. Andreas Kloden of Germany and Italian Ivan Basso were the closest competitors, but already too far back to pose any kind of serious threat.

Finally, Lance put the icing on the cake by winning the final time trial on the Saturday before the finish. That gave him five stage wins, his most ever. And when he made his sixth straight triumphant ride down the Champs-Elysées, it was a mere formality. The race was his. He won it by six minutes and nineteen seconds over Kloden, with Basso third, six minutes and forty seconds behind, and Jan Ullrich finishing fourth, some eight minutes and fifty seconds behind Lance. Lance and his U.S. Postal Service teammates had run their best race ever, and he did it despite what had now become a yearly claim that he must be using some kind of performance-enhancing drugs.

Once again he had to point out that he had never once—not one single time—tested positive for any kind of banned substance. And he was probably the most tested athlete in the world. The repeated accusations only served to fuel his motivation.

"They want to create pressure that cracks you," he said of those who continued to intimate and accuse. "So, internally, I say, 'Okay, I will never crack because of that. This will not crack me.'"

These unfounded accusations notwithstanding, his feat of winning the Tour six consecutive times was incredible. It was beginning to seem as if he simply couldn't be beaten. As fellow American rider Bobby Julich said,

"[Lance] has changed the Tour forever. He has set the blueprint for success, and he deserves all the success he is getting."

While Lance and his teammates were still celebrating what may have been their greatest victory, the speculation began. Would he be back again? Would Lance try for a seventh straight victory in 2005, when he would be close to thirty-four years old? There were certainly no more worlds to conquer when it came to the Tour de France. He had already done what no rider before him could do—win the race six times *and* in succession. He certainly didn't have anything else to prove.

Of course, even after the hoopla of victory began cooling down the questions didn't stop. Before long Lance was hinting that he might not be back for a seventh try, or perhaps skip a year, then return and try it again. He also talked about focusing on other cycling races, some of which he had been criticized for skipping in the past or simply using as a training ground for the Tour.

"I'm not saying I'll never do [the Tour] again," he said, even before the 2004 race had ended. "I'll do it again before I stop. It's a special race. It's everything. You can't have this intensity in other events. I haven't made a schedule [for next year] yet," he then added. "It's fair to say there are still a lot of things I'd like to do in cycling, like the classics and the hour record, that require a different type of focus."

Lance also was about to change sponsors. He knew already that for the 2005 season his team would switch from the U.S. Postal Service to the Discovery Channel. They had already signed a three-year, multimillion-dollar sponsorship deal, which could also affect his schedule.

"I have to discuss it with them," he said. "If they give me the green light [to compete in other races], I might do it. But if they say, 'Lance, we'd like you to do the Tour,' I understand that, too."

Even Tour officials weren't sure that Lance would return, a surprising change from the year before. After his close victory over Jan Ullrich in 2003, he immediately stated he would be back for a sixth straight year and better prepared than ever. He had certainly made good on that promise.

"[Lance] is doubtless the greatest rider ever in the Tour de France. He is proving that," said Tour president, Patrice Clerc. "Now does he want a seventh, or an eighth? I have no idea."

So that immediately became the big question. Would he or wouldn't he? During the ensuing months the rumors continued. Even the *New York Times* came out with a story that said

2004 would be the last time Lance would ride the Tour, and that he had already informed officials of his plans. The article went on to say that he saw no point in going for a seventh straight title, partially as a gesture of respect for the four cyclists who had won it five times. Yet at the same time, Discovery Channel spokesman David Leavy said that the network expected Lance to once again return to the Tour in 2005.

Johan Bruyneel, the manager of Armstrong's Discovery team and a good friend, felt the star cyclist might simply be unable to resist returning to his favorite race, especially since the Tour was his motivation the rest of the year.

Lance loved to look the naysayers directly in the eye and say, "Yes, I can!" He had been doing that for six years now. But he was also tired. As he told one reporter, "I'm more mentally than physically tired. Mentally I'm ready to go home and see my kids and relax."

And that's what he did, even skipping the Athens Olympics, held the following month, because he wanted to spend time with his children. So he prepared to leave France a champion again. Though he had never been a French favorite despite his success, he seemed to be earning respect from his obvious achievements and also some more fans.

"He's getting more *sympa*," said a French

store owner, Yves Besset, who used a French word meaning "nice" or "friendly." "At the beginning, he was cold. Now he smiles more and seems more relaxed. He's making an effort."

Many didn't understand his single-minded determination and the precise preparation that occupied his every moment from the start of the training to the finish of the race. And even though he always won, he may not have done it in the French style.

"He never hits the pedals except for a purpose," said a French journalist who covered the race regularly. "It is efficiency that he seeks, and if he attacks it is in order to win, not to please the crowd. Everything is planned with one goal in mind: to win the Tour."

Another put it more succinctly. "He rides practically. Panache is not his strong point. His business is not cycling. It's victory."

Others felt that his dominance had almost made the Tour a formality. Except for 2003, all his wins had been decided early. He had basically blown away the field in five of his six victories, usually taking charge of the race by the time the riders exited the mountains, and this rankled some fans who wanted to see more drama and competitive finishes.

"People want a spectacle, they want a close

race with suspense and upsets," said Jean-Pierre Bidet, another French journalist. "For several years now, we've been bored."

But you can't criticize an athlete for dominating his sport. In fact, it was his total dominance that Americans marveled at and the very trait that made him such an admired celebrity in his home country. It wouldn't be surprising if the French hoped he didn't return in 2005. Then they would have a wide-open race with all kinds of speculation about who would be the new champion. If Lance returned, it would be a case of "here we go again," and many would probably root for an upset just to create a new kind of excitement.

Finally, in the spring of 2005 the speculation ended. Lance announced that he would return for a seventh—and last—Tour de France. The fact that he announced that it would be his last Tour created some extra excitement. Could he, approaching his thirty-fourth birthday, win this test of will and endurance one more time? Later he would say that he announced his intention to race as soon as he made up his mind, adding, "I really thought for a while that I would skip one and then go back, but I began to worry about the age thing again. At almost thirty-four your body can start to shut down a bit. And when I didn't win any of my early races I began to wonder just how strong I'd be for the Tour."

So it wasn't so much that he abandoned his original game plan to skip a Tour or two. Rather, he began to feel the encroachment of Father Time, something every great athlete experiences at some point. He also said that his friend Eddy Merckx, whom Lance considers the greatest cyclist of all-time, returned to the Tour after winning five times and then skipping a couple, only to finish seventh in his second-to-last Tour and second in his final one. By contrast, Lance said he wanted to go out on top. "I want to end on a high note. That could be more motivating than a big bonus or making history."

There have been a large number of great athletes who have stayed too long in the game and became shells of their former selves in sports they had once dominated. That was something Lance didn't want. A former Tour teammate of Lance, Steve Bauer, felt there was no reason he couldn't win a seventh time.

"Of course he can do it again. Why shouldn't he?" Bauer said. "Maybe number seven will be the most difficult to win, but if he's in his best shape, who's going to beat him?"

One rider who vowed to try was Jan Ullrich. The German star made no secret of what drove him: to beat Lance Armstrong at his best. "My goal at the end of my career is to win the Tour again," Ullrich said, "but above all by beating Lance. I cannot imagine a victory without beating the man who has made himself the best for the last six years."

Ullrich was now part of the T-Mobile team and would have the benefit of outstanding teammates such as Andreas Kloden and Alexandre Vinokourov, both of whom vowed to help him in the mountains. As with Lance and the Discovery team, the T-Mobile team was built around Ullrich, though both Kloden and Vinokourov had the skills to make a run at Lance, as well.

It had been a strange year. Lance raced very little so that he could prepare for the Tour, so no one really knew what kind of shape he would be in. When he finished fourth at the Dauphine Libere, which was considered a final warm-up race for the Tour, there was more speculation. Would it be 2003 again, or would he still dominate? Jeremy Whittle, the editor of *ProCycling* magazine, felt Lance was ready.

"Three months ago I'd have said someone else would win [the Tour]," Whittle said. "Now I think Armstrong will do it again. He is exactly where he wants to be in terms of fitness."

Finally it was race time. It didn't take long

for those in the know to see that Lance was ready. He didn't win the opening time trial, but he immediately opened a gap of nearly one minute over Ullrich. He then used his guile and skills in the early stages, avoiding trouble and potential crashes, and staying close to the lead. He also made sure, as he always did, to keep his main rivals behind him. It was as if he had built-in radar to know just who was where and how fast he would have to go to keep them there—behind him.

In the mountains, beginning with Stage Ten, Lance made his move. He did it on the punishing 13.8-mile climb to the ski station of Courchevel, seeming to ride uphill with ease as most of his rivals—notably Ullrich—struggled and grimaced in pain. Spain's Alejando Valverdo just beat Lance to the finish line, though they finished with the same time. More importantly, Lance now had the yellow jersey. Mickael Rasmussen of Denmark was thirty-eight seconds behind Lance, but not considered a main challenger, while the dangerous Ivan Basso was third, two minutes and forty seconds behind his American rival. As for Ullrich, he was already four minutes and two seconds behind, a very large margin at that point in the race.

"Today, I had good legs," Lance said. "We

169

are in a good position with regards to some of the main rivals, so we'll have to protect that. There's still a lot of racing to go. I don't think [Ullrich and Vinokourov] are finished. I am going to be the last person to write them off. They are going to make life difficult and we'll continue to watch them and continue to respect them."

No one was better at protecting a lead than Lance. Yes, he was aware of his rivals and did expect them to make a move. But he was always ready to answer any attack with a counterattack of his own. He held the lead. By the time the riders came out of the mountains, it looked as if the inevitable was about to happen again. Lance Armstrong, still wearing the yellow jersey, was on his way to a seventh straight Tour de France victory. Unlike 2004, when he took five individual stages, Lance hadn't yet won a single stage. But that didn't matter. It was total time that counted, and his numbers remained lower than all the rest.

Finally, during another time trail in the second-to-last stage, Lance put the icing on the cake. Instead of riding conservatively to maintain his lead, he went all out, peddling furiously from beginning to end and winning the stage while increasing his lead at the same time. It was all but over. The final ride down the

Champs-Elysées was shortened by bad weather, but it didn't matter. Lance was in total control. He had won a seventh straight Tour de France. Once again, he won it without much drama and with relative ease. Basso was second, four minutes and forty seconds behind Lance, and Ullrich, the rider many felt had the best chance to dethrone the king, was third—six minutes and twenty-one seconds behind Lance. Lance Armstrong showed once again than he owned the greatest bicycle race in the world, and that he had, indeed, gone out on top.

Standing tall on the podium for a seventh time, Lance was gracious in victory. He was savoring the moment because he knew it was the last time he would ever be standing there. He praised both his teammates and his rivals.

"I couldn't have done this without the team behind me," he said. "I owe them everything. [Jan] Ullrich is a special rival and a special person, and Basso is almost too good of a friend to race. He may be the future of the Tour." Then, alluding to the always-nearby speculation about illegal drugs, he added, "You should believe this, these people [the cyclists]. There are no secrets. This is a hard Tour and hard work wins it.

"Vive le Tour."

So it was finally over. The great comeback from cancer that began in 1999 had culminated with seven years of dominance in arguably the world's most difficult sporting event. It is still difficult to put Lance's unique accomplishment into words. He not only left an indelible mark on his sport, but was one of the greatest to ever grace it. Before long, others in the sport were talking about the man who had set new standards for the Tour de France.

"We can say that he has been the best cyclist of his generation," said the former Spanish champion Miguel Indurain. "But we shouldn't make the error of comparing his achievements to other eras as each one is different and each has its own peculiarities. . . . There are many ways to retire from the sport, but Lance has chosen the most brilliant as he has retired as a great champion without having encountered a rival who could defeat him."

Indurain added, "As for the future [of the Tour], I think there will be two or three more open races where a lot of leaders will compete ferociously for the triumph until another dominant leader emerges to establish a new era. Sooner or later a rider will emerge who will win more Tours. In every sport we have seen how the records eventually get broken and cycling is no exception."

Still, it's hard to picture any one athlete duplicating Lance Armstrong's feats. In

America he was considered a hero of epic proportions, not only because of his cycling accomplishments, but for his humanitarian work as well. Former teammate Jonathan Vaughters, who had moved on to coaching junior riders in the United States, spoke for many when he said, "He's a once-in-a-lifetime athlete. I don't know if I will live to see, or my son will live to see, anyone like him again."

Those sentiments were seconded by another friend and teammate, George Hincapie, when he said, "Everybody is looking for the next Lance, but there won't be another Lance for another century."

But what's next for Lance? His racing career may be over, but he is not the kind of guy who will disappear into obscurity. Immediately following the race he took his children and girlfriend, Sheryl Crow, for a vacation, but before leaving the site of his seven triumphs, he told a reporter, "I'm an athlete. I'm not going to sit around and be a fat slob. I don't know the next time I'll ride a bike. I've got to refocus my life and try to find a new balance. I need goals, but they won't be sporting goals. I can't imagine a life of vacation, but I can imagine one with more vacations. I still want to try to make a difference in the world."

Part of that difference will be continuing his

work with the Lance Armstrong Foundation and leading the fight against cancer. He is totally committed to it. The yellow LIVE-STRONG bracelets are so popular, they have spawned copycats for other causes. He works in conjunction with the National Cancer Institute and has said that his personal goal is to eliminate the suffering and death from cancer by 2015. Of course, more money is needed and that's where Lance can help. His energies and talents are perfect for fund-raising activities, and his celebrity status brought on by his seven Tour wins and incredible personal story should keep him in a high-profile and public position.

And then there's politics. There have already been rumors that Lance may seek public office either in or from his home state of Texas. Answering one of many questions about his future, this one touching on politics, Lance said, "I'm a fighter, and I do have certain beliefs. I don't think I'm truly cut out for [politics], but if people want it in ten years, who knows?"

No matter how you look at his career, his battle with cancer remains the fulcrum around which everything revolves. He was an excellent cyclist before his illness; one of the best ever after it. He wasn't a very good stage-race cyclist before; perhaps the best ever after cancer. As with everything else in his life, Lance Armstrong can now put his illness and what it gave him in perspective. He said, "[Cancer] put pain in perspective for me, it put suffering and defeat in perspective. The illness taught me how to really suffer and suffer slowly, and it's not as if you get sick and it hurts and a week later you get better. It's a long type of suffering, physical, emotional, mental, social. It gave me a certain sense of hunger and drive and determination that I was going to come back and give it my all."

On the bike or off it, Lance Armstrong has been giving it his all ever since.

Biography

Bill Gutman has written more than two hundred books for children and adults in a writing career spanning more than thirty years. His most recent books are *Twice Around the Bases*, written with former Texas Rangers and Boston Red Sox manager and current FOX broadcaster Kevin Kennedy; and *It's Outta Here! The History of the Home Run from Babe Ruth to Barry Bonds*. His previous biography subjects for Simon & Schuster include Michael Jordan, Tiger Woods, Brett Favre, Ken Griffey Jr., Sammy Sosa, Grant Hill, Shaquille O'Neal, and Marion Jones. Mr. Gutman lives in upstate New York, with his wife, Cathy.